Christian Heroes: Then & Now

WILFRED GRENFELL

Fisher of Men

CHRISTIAN HEROES: THEN & NOW

WILFRED GRENFELL

Fisher of Men

JANET & GEOFF BENGE

YWAM Publishing is the publishing ministry of Youth With A Mission (YWAM), an international missionary organization of Christians from many denominations dedicated to presenting Jesus Christ to this generation. To this end, YWAM has focused its efforts in three main areas: (1) training and equipping believers for their part in fulfilling the Great Commission (Matthew 28:19), (2) personal evangelism, and (3) mercy ministry (medical and relief work).

To learn more about our books and materials, call (425) 771-1153 or (800) 922-2143 or email books@ywampublishing.com. Visit us online at www.ywampublishing.com.

Wilfred Grenfell: Fisher of Men
Copyright © 2003 by YWAM Publishing

Published by YWAM Publishing
a ministry of Youth With A Mission
P.O. Box 55787, Seattle, WA 98155

All rights reserved. No part of this book may be reproduced in any form without permission in writing from the publisher, except in the case of brief quotations in critical articles or reviews.

ISBN 978-1-57658-292-3 (paperback)
ISBN 978-1-57658-612-9 (e-book)

Library of Congress Cataloging-in-Publication Data
Benge, Janet, 1958–
    Wilfred Grenfell : fisher of men / by Janet and Geoff Benge.
      p. cm.—(Christian heroes, then & now)
Includes bibliographical references.
    ISBN 1-57658-292-2
    1. Grenfell, Wilfred Thomason, Sir, 1865-1940—Juvenile literature.
2. Missionaries, Medical—Newfoundland and Labrador—Juvenile literature. [1. Grenfell, Wilfred Thomason, Sir, 1865-1940. 2. Missionaries. 3. Physicians.] I. Benge, Geoff, 1954- II. Title. III. Series.
    R722.32.G75B46 2003
      610'.92—dc21   2003008863

Sixth printing 2025

Printed in the United States of America

CHRISTIAN HEROES: THEN & NOW

Adoniram Judson	Isobel Kuhn
Albert Schweitzer	Jacob DeShazer
Amy Carmichael	Jim Elliot
Betty Greene	John Flynn
Brother Andrew	John Newton
Cameron Townsend	John Wesley
Charles Mulli	John Williams
Clarence Jones	Jonathan Goforth
Corrie ten Boom	Klaus-Dieter John
Count Zinzendorf	Lillian Trasher
C. S. Lewis	Loren Cunningham
C. T. Studd	Lottie Moon
David Bussau	Mary Slessor
David Livingstone	Mildred Cable
Dietrich Bonhoeffer	Nate Saint
D. L. Moody	Norman Grubb
Elisabeth Elliot	Paul Brand
Eric Liddell	Rachel Saint
Florence Young	Richard Wurmbrand
Francis Asbury	Rowland Bingham
George Müller	Samuel Zwemer
Gladys Aylward	Sundar Singh
Helen Roseveare	Wilfred Grenfell
Hudson Taylor	William Booth
Ida Scudder	William Carey

Available in paperback, e-book, and audiobook formats. Unit study curriculum guides are available for select biographies.

www.YWAMpublishing.com

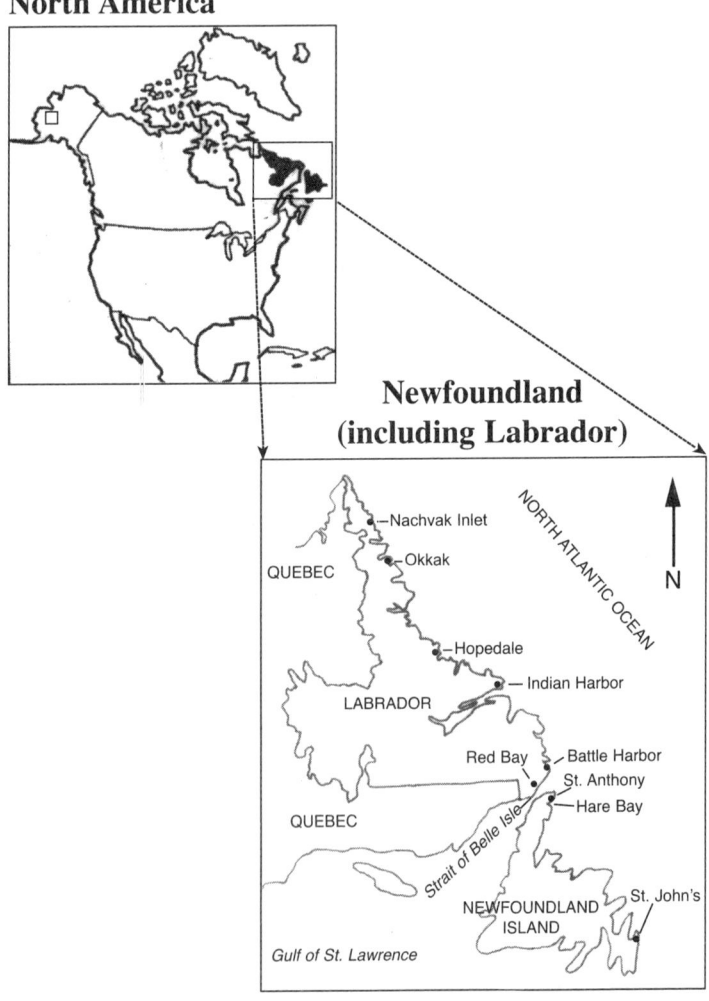

Contents

1. So This Is How It's All Going to End!........ 9
2. The Sands of Dee 13
3. New Direction........................... 25
4. Something Quite Different 39
5. On the North Sea 47
6. Labrador................................ 59
7. Back to Labrador........................ 73
8. A Growing Mission 85
9. Pomiuk................................ 101
10. Seal Hunt 117
11. Red Bay Cooperative Society 125
12. A Single Letter Changed Everything 135
13. Adrift 147
14. International Grenfell Association........ 159
15. Knight Commander of St. Michael and St. George........................ 169
16. Home at Last.......................... 181
    Bibliography 191

Chapter 1

So This Is How It's All Going to End!

The icy cold stabbed at Wilfred Grenfell's fingers and toes like a knife. He wished he could warm his hands and feet by a fire, but there was nothing to burn out here, and even if there were, his matches had gotten wet when the dogsled went through the ice. It was dark now, and his damp clothes were frozen to his body. Even covering himself with the dogskin blanket and snuggling up to his biggest sled dog, Doc, were not enough to keep out the sharp edge of the Arctic cold.

The wind was still howling from the northwest, pushing the ice pan he was stranded on out to sea—and with it hope of rescue. Beyond the bay was the angry, turbulent water of the North Atlantic.

Now, in late winter, it gobbled up the chunks of broken up pack ice as they drifted out of the bays. And as the sea pounded the ice pans to pieces, anything stranded on them, such as Wilfred and his six remaining dogs, would be tossed into the frigid ocean, where death would come quickly.

Wilfred tried to dismiss the thought from his mind. It did no good to think on such things. Besides, he reminded himself, he had been stranded on the ice pan now for well over twelve hours, and he was still alive. Maybe there was room for hope. But the cold was his enemy. He could feel the strength seeping from his bones, and he knew from his medical training that his body was descending into hypothermic shock.

Wilfred rubbed his frozen hands together to generate some warmth and thought about how he had gotten here. He had been on his way from St. Anthony, on the northern tip of Newfoundland, to Brent Island, on the southern edge of Hare Bay sixty miles south of St. Anthony. He had spent last night at Lock's Cove on the northern edge of Hare Bay and set out from there at first light. But it was late winter, and in the night the wind had begun to break up the pack ice. The locals had warned him not to try crossing the pack ice on the bay, the shortest distance to Brent Island, because it was unsafe. They had urged him to follow the coastline to his destination. And that is what he had done. He had followed the coastline for several miles until he noticed an ice bridge to an uninhabited island in Hare Bay. If he crossed the ice bridge to the island and then crossed the narrow sheet of ice between the island and the south shore of the bay, he would cut miles off his journey and so get to his patient, a boy suffering from blood poisoning, sooner. He took the risk and headed out onto the ice bridge. But what looked like solid ice from shore turned out to be soft, gooey sish ice. Partway to the island, the dogsled began to sink. Wilfred had had to cut the dogs free and abandon the sled, which quickly sank all the way through the ice. Wilfred and the nine dogs had made it to an ice pan, where they were now stranded and drifting out to sea.

When the afternoon shadows had stretched long across the bay and the temperature had begun to plummet, Wilfred knew he had to do more to stay warm through the night. He'd had to do the unthinkable. He had killed and skinned three of his dogs. Their hides now made up the blanket he was huddled under, providing some shelter from the icy, bone-chilling wind. But he was losing the battle with the cold. He had dozed for a while, afraid that if he slept too long, he would never wake up. He thought he saw the sun rising, but when he looked closer, it was a bright, full moon peeking through the clouds above.

Wilfred snuggled closer beside Doc, trying to absorb every bit of excess heat the hulking dog produced. As he tried to drift off to sleep once again, the words of a hymn that he had sung as a boy back in Parkgate, England, began to play over in his mind.

> My God, my Father, while I stray
> Far from my home on life's dark way,
> Oh, teach me from my heart to say,
> Thy will be done!

After a few minutes, Wilfred opened his eyes and looked up at the moon. *So this is how it's all going to end,* he thought to himself. *How fitting that I should die on the ocean.* His mind drifted back to his earliest memories as a child; they were of the sea. He had spent his whole life on or around the ocean. How he wished he were back in Parkgate right now, sailing on the estuary of the River Dee in the *Reptile* with his older brother Algernon. What a strange path his life had taken from those times, that he should find himself adrift on an ice pan off the Newfoundland coast, headed for certain death.

Chapter 2

The Sands of Dee

"Wilfred," the English teacher said, tapping his cane on the blackboard, "would you stand and recite the *Sands of Dee* to the class, please."

Ten-year-old Wilfred Grenfell pushed his chair back and stood. He hated reciting in front of the class, but there was no way out of it, not when his father was the principal and his mother the school bookkeeper and discipline recorder. Anytime he set a foot wrong in class, they both knew about it within minutes!

It wasn't that reciting poetry was difficult for Wilfred. In fact, anything that involved memorization was simple for him. It was just that he did not particularly like being the center of attention. Still, he took a deep breath and began:

O Mary, go and call the cattle home,
And call the cattle home,
And call the cattle home,
Across the sands o' Dee:
The western wind was wild and dank wi' foam;
And all alone went she.

The western tide crept up along the sand,
And o'er and o'er the sand,
And round and round the sand,
As far as eye could see;
The blinding mist came down and hid the land:
And never home came she.

Wilfred paused to briefly look around the classroom and then continued.

Oh! is it weed or fish, or floating hair—
A tress of golden hair,
O' drowned maiden's hair,
Above the nets at sea?
Was never salmon yet that shone so fair,
Among the stakes on Dee.

They rowed her in across the rolling foam,
The cruel, crawling foam,
The cruel, hungry foam,
To her grave beside the sea;
But still the boatmen hear her call the cattle home,
Across the sands o' Dee.

"Very good, very good," the teacher said. "It will be your turn to recite a poem tomorrow, James. Now open your books to page fifty-three, and let's look at the rhyming couplets in the next poem."

Wilfred dutifully turned to the page, but his eyes soon drifted across the room and out the window. It was odd, but he was staring out at the sands of Dee, the exact scene described in the poem. His father's cousin, a famous English poet named Charles Kingsley, had written the poem, in part to warn people about the treacherous waters of the River Dee estuary. Not that Wilfred needed a poem to remind him. He had walked out on the sandy stretch that separated his village of Parkgate, Cheshire, England, from the Welsh peninsula, for as long as he could remember. Only last year he had watched helplessly as an old fisherman got caught by the swiftly incoming tide and was swept out to sea and to his death. Unlike Mary in the poem, his body had never been recovered.

But the dangers of the estuary, with its quicksand, swift-flowing channel nicknamed "The Deep," and rapid changes in weather, did not stop Wilfred or Algernon from venturing out on it every day. Just looking at the pictures and artifacts that adorned the walls of Mostyn House School reminded Wilfred that he came from a long line of courageous adventurers.

In the great hall were twelve stuffed animal heads—tigers, leopards, and deer—all from India. Wilfred's grandfather Hutchinson had been a colonel in the British army stationed in India. Wilfred's mother had been born and raised there, and most of her family still lived in India. No fewer than fifty of her cousins served in the army or civil service.

Often, when Wilfred gazed into the eyes of the animals in the great hall, he imagined his relatives stalking their prey through tall grass and across marshy lowlands. When no one was watching, he and Algernon pretended they were big-game hunters, though their prey was more likely to be an oyster catcher or a sandpiper, and their gun a broomstick.

Lots of paintings also hung on the walls of the school. They were mainly of people from his father's side of the family. About fifty years before, his grandfather had changed the spelling of their last name from Grenville to Grenfell, but his Grenville ancestors were well worth remembering. There was Basil Grenville, commander of the Cornish army that fought for King Charles. And Wilfred's great-uncle, John Pascoe Grenville, had gone to sea at eleven years of age. As a young man, he had fought with the Chilean navy, helping it defeat the Spanish navy. With sword in hand, he had been the first man aboard the *Esmeralda*, the Spanish admiral's ship, when the Chileans stormed and captured the vessel. From there he had gone on to serve in the Brazilian navy in the war with Portugal. He rose to the rank of rear admiral and was then made Brazil's ambassador to London. However, Wilfred could not remember this uncle, who had died in London in 1869, when Wilfred was only four years old.

Once school was dismissed for the day, Wilfred went to find his mother, who was normally in the school office, bent over a tally book. His younger brother, five-year-old Cecil, often sat beside her playing with a toy train.

"Hello, Cecil," Wilfred said as he bent down to pat his brother on the shoulder.

Cecil looked up and smiled. It was a rare sight. There had been complications when he was born, and his brain did not function properly. Everyone at school knew that Cecil was never to be left alone because he could easily hurt himself.

Within minutes twelve-year-old Algernon tumbled into the office. The boys' mother pulled out a basket of shortbread and gave each boy a piece.

"So how was school today?" she asked.

As usual Algernon was the one who answered the question. "Great. I came top in the Latin quiz again, and Master Myers says I can move on to the next chapter in my French book."

"Wonderful," Mrs. Grenfell replied. "And how about you, Wilfred?"

"Fine," he muttered. Although his grades were just as good as his older brother's, it was Algernon and not Wilfred who loved to study and learn from books. Wilfred would much rather be outdoors. He was grateful that summer vacation was only a week away.

Wilfred was particularly looking forward to the break. Every summer his parents went to the Swiss Alps, leaving their three sons in the care of the school matron. Always preoccupied with keeping Cecil safe, she let Algernon and Wilfred roam freely all summer long. And this year was especially exciting. Their father had given Wilfred and Algernon permission to build a boat!

As the semester came to a close, Wilfred went over in his head every detail of the boat. It had to have a shallow draft so that they could explore the salt marshes farther up the estuary and a square stern to make it sturdy in the ocean waves of the Irish Sea.

The two boys had saved their pocket money all year and had enough to buy the planks and nails they needed. It had not been hard for them to convince their father to hire the village carpenter to supervise the project. Their father seemed happy to indulge his sons' passion for the ocean. Because Cheshire's weather could be unpredictable, even in summer, the boys had also convinced their father to allow them to build the boat in a second-story classroom. When she was finished, they intended to lower her slowly out the window, slide her down the sloping first-story roof, and then lower her to the ground.

Building the boat was a long, exacting task. The planks had to be cut and shaped with chisels and planes and then attached to the frame. But bit by bit the boat slowly took shape, until it was time to move her outside to paint. As they lowered her to the ground, Wilfred had to admit to himself that she looked like no other boat he had ever seen, part punt, part canoe. In fact, she looked more like a floating coffin than a boat. But Wilfred did not mind. He knew that despite her strange appearance, she would be one of the most seaworthy boats on the estuary.

Once the boat was safely on the ground, Wilfred and Algernon painted her red and christened her the *Reptile*. For the rest of the summer, the boys were seldom home. They paddled up and down the river, taking turns diving overboard and being bobbed along by the swift current of "the Deep." The current, with its swirls and eddies, would often carry one of them to the Welsh shore, leaving the other brother to maneuver the *Reptile* after him to pick him up.

Algernon had a hunting rifle, and the boys often shot wild birds and brought them home for the cook to prepare for dinner. An old sailor in the village had taught Wilfred how to stuff and mount some of the birds he caught. Soon Wilfred had an impressive collection of stuffed birds lined up along the sill of his bedroom window.

Many times over the summer Wilfred and Algernon did not make it home at all. They stayed out all night working alongside the fishermen of Parkgate, hauling in nets and scaling fish for the market.

This was the life Wilfred enjoyed most—pitting himself against nature and testing his endurance.

Summer came to an end, however, and the *Reptile* had to be exchanged for schoolbooks. Still, Wilfred had next summer to dream about, and the summer after that. In fact, he imagined he would spend his entire life in Parkgate and on the water that surrounded the village.

It came as a shock, then, in 1879, when Wilfred's father called him into his office and announced that Wilfred was to be sent off to Marlborough College in Wiltshire. Marlborough was a famous school dedicated to training the sons of clergymen. Although Wilfred's father, Algernon Grenfell, had been a schoolmaster all his working life, he was also an ordained minister.

A week later, looking back on the shocking announcement, Wilfred realized he should have expected to be sent off to school. His brother Algernon was already away at a different boarding school, but somehow it had never occurred to Wilfred that he would follow in his older brother's footsteps.

After the summer vacation of 1879, Wilfred set out for the Wiltshire countryside, two hundred miles southeast of Parkgate.

After a long day of traveling by train, Wilfred found himself looking up at Marlborough Castle. This previous home of the dukes of Somerset now housed the high school he would be attending. The castle was surrounded by a moat, which had been widened in one spot to make a swimming hole. Wilfred smiled to himself; at least there was some water in the vicinity.

Life soon fell into a dull pattern for Wilfred. He disliked most of the other boys in his class and soon earned the nickname "the Beast" because he did not comb his hair unless he was forced to and often fought with the other boys. The truth was, Wilfred was bored. The things the other boys considered daring exploits seemed tame to him. The bravest of the boys would climb out the window in the dead of night and go swimming in the moat pool. But Wilfred recalled the numerous times he had thrown himself overboard from the *Reptile* and pitted his strength against the roaring tide at the mouth of the River Dee. Or the times he had stayed out all night hauling wet nets filled with fish over the stern of a thirty-foot fishing boat. He recalled watching grown men get tangled in the nets and be pulled overboard to their deaths.

Wilfred liked to be by himself most of the time, and Sunday was his favorite day of the week. The day started with chapel service. While the drone of the chaplain's voice often nearly put Wilfred to sleep, after the sermon the boys always sang the entire work of Handel's *Messiah*. Even though many people had told Wilfred he was tone deaf—"unitone," they dubbed him—he loved to sing loudly, and he did so with gusto.

After chapel the boys were supposed to return to their rooms for silent reading or letter writing. This was when Wilfred would often sneak away to nearby Savernake Forest and catch moths and butterflies. It was a poor substitute for shooting curlews, plovers, and terns on the River Dee estuary, but at least he was alone out in nature.

Two years dragged by at Marlborough College, until Wilfred convinced his father that he was so unhappy there that he needed to be brought home.

Now, in 1881, Wilfred was back enjoying the life he loved. His father made him keep studying Greek, Latin, and mathematics, but apart from that, Wilfred was free to roam as he pleased. He lost no time in climbing aboard a fishing boat and heading out into the Irish Sea in pursuit of a catch. Meanwhile Algernon had stuck with his studies and was now enrolled in university at Oxford.

Wilfred's happy and carefree life lasted for almost a year, until his father called him into his office once again.

"Shut the door after you," Mr. Grenfell said softly. He cleared his throat. "I have something to tell you that may come as a shock. Sit down."

Wilfred perched on the edge of a leather chair and waited, wondering what his father could possibly have to say that would be earth-shattering.

"Your mother and I have been very happy here at Parkgate," Wilfred's father began. "The school is going well and gaining a fine reputation, and we have raised you boys here. But that life is about to come to an end. After much soul searching, I have accepted a post as chaplain at the London Hospital in Whitechapel Road."

Wilfred gasped. He had read enough of Charles Dickens's works to know that Whitechapel Road was the worst slum area in all of London!

"You mean you are leaving here for good and moving to London?" Wilfred asked, almost unable to comprehend such a thought.

"Yes, we are," his father said. "I have already written to Algernon, and when he graduates he is going to come back here and run the school. In the meantime I have found a deputy who will keep it running. I'll come back every three months or so to make sure everything is going well. Now we have to talk about you."

"Me? What about me?" Wilfred asked.

"Well...what do you want to do with your life, son? You will have to earn a living."

The question struck Wilfred with the force of a huge breaker. He had never considered that he would have to earn his own way in life. Boys of his social standing took up professions if and when they found them interesting. If need be, they could live indefinitely off family money.

"I...I..." Wilfred sputtered, but he could not think of a single way to continue the sentence.

After a long silence, his father finally spoke.

"I know this may all be somewhat of a shock to you. You don't have to answer me now, but you do have to think seriously about it. I am taking up my new appointment in November, and I would like to have you positioned by then."

Wilfred gulped. That was only three months away.

After he left his father's office, Wilfred wandered along the water's edge, wondering with each step how he was supposed to work out what he wanted to do for the rest of his life.

Chapter 3

New Direction

For the next twenty-four hours, Wilfred was in a daze. Earn a living! What could he do, not just for a while but year after year? As he wandered through the school late at night, his eyes turned, as they had a thousand times before, to the stuffed animal trophies mounted on the walls. In a flash, inspiration hit him. He would be a tiger hunter in India! That way he could meet all of his mother's relatives and live an adventure-filled life. The more he thought about it, the more seventeen-year-old Wilfred liked the idea. Algernon could lead the life of a dull schoolteacher if he wanted, but Wilfred would stalk dangerous prey in the tall grasses of the subcontinent of India.

When Wilfred confided his idea to his mother, however, she arranged for him to talk to a friend, the wife of a missionary who had lived in India. The woman now lived in a nearby town, so Wilfred climbed on his bicycle and rode over to visit her. He was eager to talk over his idea with her, but the result of the conversation was disheartening. The woman, Mrs. Jamison, explained to Wilfred that tiger hunting was a hobby very rich Englishmen indulged in. A real tiger hunt cost thousands of pounds, and there was no way to recuperate the money spent. Neither Wilfred nor anyone else could make a good living in India hunting tigers.

Mrs. Jamison had another suggestion for Wilfred. Perhaps, she suggested, he could become a clergyman or a missionary. Wilfred did not like to say anything insulting, but these two options were the furthest thing from his mind. Nothing on earth sounded more boring!

As he rode home to Parkgate, Wilfred became increasingly frustrated. A young man of his class could not become a fisherman or learn a trade; it simply was not done. Yet the kinds of jobs his social rank suited him for seemed tedious. A gloomy silence settled over him.

When he got home, Wilfred's father was waiting for him.

"How did it go?" he asked.

Wilfred shrugged his shoulders. "Apparently there isn't any money in tiger hunting, not enough to live on, anyway. Mrs. Jamison suggested I might want to become a clergyman or a missionary, but I can't see myself doing that for the rest of my life."

"In that case, I have another suggestion for you. Why don't you go and talk to Dr. Sharples? You might find doctoring interesting work."

Wilfred nodded. "I'll go in the morning. Perhaps I would like being a doctor."

As Wilfred thought about it, he realized that he knew little of being a doctor. All he knew was that Dr. Sharples had a wide-ranging practice and spent many hours a week on horseback traveling from patient to patient. That alone made the job sound appealing, and Wilfred left in good spirits the following morning to find the doctor.

Dr. Sharples had not yet begun his morning rounds when Wilfred arrived, and he welcomed the young man into his office.

"Your father told me you might be by," the doctor said. "Now tell me, what is this about your thinking of becoming a doctor?"

Wilfred felt himself turning red. He was interested in what a doctor did, but he wasn't seriously thinking about becoming one.

Dr. Sharples chatted away to Wilfred about medical training, about what books to read, and about some of the things he liked most about his job. Wilfred sat listening with polite interest until Dr. Sharples got up and went to a shelf, from which he lifted down a large jar with a lid on it.

"See this?" he said, placing the jar beside Wilfred. "This is the key to the entire human body. Do you know what it is, lad?"

Wilfred gazed at the gray, jellylike blob floating inside the jar.

"No, sir," he replied.

"It's a brain, a human brain."

Wilfred leaned forward and studied it intently.

"Take a good look at it," Dr. Sharples continued. "Things go on in there that we can only guess at. What we do know is that the brain sends messages down the spinal cord that dictate every movement we make. The brain constantly assesses what the body is doing and makes adjustments."

Wilfred continued to stare at the pickled brain. It had never before occurred to him to think of the human body as a finely tuned machine. He had studied anatomy at Marlborough College, but seeing a real brain in front of him, rather than one sketched in a stuffy textbook, opened a whole new world to him.

Wilfred spent another twenty minutes talking with Dr. Sharples before heading home. He decided to walk home the long way, via the sandy shoreline. He told himself that he needed time to think before seeing his parents. But in reality Wilfred had already made up his mind—he would become a doctor and explore the intricacies of the human body.

When Wilfred told his father of his decision, Mr. Grenfell was delighted. He gave Wilfred the choice of going to Oxford to get his medical degree or moving to London with the rest of the family and studying at London Hospital Medical School. It did not take Wilfred long to make up his mind; he wanted to go to London with his parents and Cecil.

Once his mind was made up, time flew by, and in early November 1882, the Grenfells packed up their belongings and set out for London.

The city was very different from living by the sea in Parkgate. The streets were full of noise and people and horses and buggies and hansom cabs. Crumbling brick buildings lined both sides of the streets, blocking the sun and providing corners for all manner of garbage and human waste to gather. Even walking down to the London docks to be near water again was a disappointing experience. The water of the River Thames was putrid. It was a dark gray-brown color and so thick that Wilfred marveled that it actually flowed. And then there was the stench that stung his nostrils. Wilfred longed for the water of the River Dee as it flowed through the estuary into the sea.

By Wilfred's eighteenth birthday on February 28, 1883, he was two weeks into his medical training and already very disappointed with what he saw. Older students told him that the London Hospital Medical School, which was actually part of London University, was no better or worse than most other medical schools in England. But Wilfred was dismayed by the experience. He had botany class first thing on Monday morning. At the first lecture, one student spilled a solution of carbon disulfide at the front of the room, and the smell of rotten eggs was so strong that the lecture had to be cancelled. The second Monday someone brought two pigeons to class and let them loose. Peashooters were passed around, and the students climbed on the desks trying to shoot the birds down from the rafters.

After that experience Wilfred decided not to bother attending any more botany classes. Instead he paid the record keeper who sat at the door recording attendance to mark him present. He did the same in many of his other classes, too, although he did like chemistry class, where the students concocted many flavors of eggnog.

He studied at home when he felt like it and relied on the old system of crammers to get him through his exams when the time came. Crammers were men who had been around the university for many years. They knew each of the professors, their pet subjects, and many of the questions that recurred in the tests they wrote. Some crammers, it was rumored, even paid professors for an advance copy of the exam papers.

Knowing that he could hire a crammer at the end of the semester, Wilfred felt at liberty to fill his university days doing the things he liked best: playing all kinds of sports. With so much spare time, he set out on an intense course of bodybuilding. He soon made the London University rowing team, the boxing team, both the university and the Richmond rugby teams, and the cricket team. His life had never been so much fun!

Wilfred was often up at the crack of dawn, plunging into the Serpentine River for a morning swim. Even on days when sheets of ice covered the water, he broke through the ice and jumped in anyway, enjoying the invigorating experience. It did not take long for him to make quite a name for himself as an excellent athlete.

With the help of a crammer, Wilfred passed his first semester exams. Then it was off to Parkgate for the summer holidays. It was a breath of fresh air to be at home by the water again. Algernon had just graduated from Oxford and returned to become the principal of Mostyn House School. However, all work was forgotten as the two brothers bought an old fishing trawler and refurbished her. Then they took her out into the Irish Sea on fishing excursions. At times Wilfred seriously considered ditching his studies and staying in Parkgate. But then he would remind himself that his father expected him to get a job and earn a living.

Thankfully, the second semester of medical studies was more engaging for Wilfred than the first. Second semester students were allowed to follow the doctors as they made their rounds of patients. London Hospital, with its nine hundred beds, was one of the largest and most diverse hospitals in the country. Wilfred was assigned to Dr. Fredrick Treves, who, although he was only thirty years old, was already well-known as a brilliant surgeon. Wilfred soon discovered that Dr. Treves was a strict and exacting mentor who followed the revolutionary ideas of Joseph Lister. Lister believed that infection was passed from person to person by invisible germs and that doctors who came in contact with an infectious person had to be very careful not to get those germs on themselves and transfer them to other patients. To ensure that these germs were not passed on, Lister promoted the application of purified carbolic acid on wounds to kill germs. He also insisted that surgical instruments and the surgeon's hands be sterilized with carbolic acid before and after surgery.

Many of the doctors and students at London Hospital thought the idea of sterilizing things was a passing fad, but not Dr. Treves. He insisted that his students wear spotless frock coats and wash their hands after touching a patient. At first Wilfred found this tedious, but when he heard that many of the patients Dr. Treves had amputated limbs from had actually lived to go home, he changed his opinion. And when Wilfred learned that the doctor was also an avid sportsman, he grew to admire him even more.

Now Wilfred found that he wanted to attend classes and even go on house calls around the hospital. London Hospital was located in the middle of a slum. In fact, many of those who lived around the hospital did not even have a roof over their heads or anywhere to sleep. Thirty-three thousand people were homeless in the area, and another fifty thousand lived in workhouses. Because these people were so poor, the medical students were encouraged to practice their doctoring skills on them free of charge. It was after one of these house calls that Wilfred experienced something that would change him forever.

In the fall of 1884, during his fourth semester, Wilfred was called out to a maternity case in one of the poorest parts of the East End of London. He helped the woman deliver a puny baby, talked to her about keeping her hands clean when she handled the child, and then left. As he started the walk back to the hospital, Wilfred decided to take a different route than usual. He turned left and headed down a dimly lit street in Shadwell. A few minutes later he found himself confronted by a most unusual sight. Right in the middle of a trash-filled vacant lot someone had set up a huge red-and-white striped tent. The back of the tent was open to the night air, and as Wilfred walked slowly past, he could see hundreds of poor people sitting quietly. This seemed almost more extraordinary to Wilfred than the sight of the tent itself. He had never seen such a rabble of poor people behaving so courteously. He simply had to find out what was going on.

Wilfred stood at the back of the tent. Looking over the rows of people, he saw a powerful-looking man at the front. The man was standing on a low stage, and somewhere to his left someone else was talking—no, praying, Wilfred decided. As he listened to the prayer, which seemed to never end, Wilfred remembered that the famous American preacher D. L. Moody was holding meetings in London. Of course, he told himself, this was one of those rip-roaring American evangelistic meetings that were being reported on in the press. Wilfred stood at the back for another two minutes as the long prayer continued. Finally his curiosity was satisfied, and Wilfred turned to leave. It was then that he heard Moody's booming voice.

"Let us sing a hymn while our brother finishes his prayer. Number twenty-three, 'Rock of Ages.'"

As the hymn began, drowning out the man's lengthy prayer, Wilfred laughed aloud. He had to admire the way Moody had moved the program forward.

A boy seated in the back row moved over and beckoned for Wilfred to sit down. Wilfred slipped into the seat. Soon the hymn was over, and D. L. Moody began to preach. Something about the message hit home with Wilfred, and though he did not go forward as Moody urged all "sinners" to do, he had plenty to think about that night. Despite the thousands of times he had been to church over the years, it was the first time Wilfred felt that he understood the gospel message.

As the weeks went by, however, Wilfred's love of sports eventually crowded out his thoughts about God, and Moody's words slowly dimmed in his mind.

Wilfred also had something else to occupy his mind. His father was sick, so sick, in fact, that he gave up his position at the hospital and was placed in a private nursing home in North Wales. Wilfred's mother stayed in a boarding house nearby and visited her husband every day. Unfortunately there was little anyone could do, and the Reverend Algernon Grenfell died in January 1885.

It was a devastating blow to Wilfred, who found himself remembering D. L. Moody's words once again. Then, a few days after his father's funeral, Wilfred spotted a poster announcing that Moody was back in London, this time with a group of young men dubbed the "Cambridge Seven." Every eager young sports fan in England knew about the Cambridge Seven—seven young men from wealthy homes who had each distinguished himself in sports or military service. One of the group had played cricket for England, other members had been on the Oxford rowing team, and one had been a dragoon guardsman and an officer in the royal artillery. Each of these seven men had turned the idea of missionary upside down by volunteering to work in China with Hudson Taylor and his China Inland Mission. Some people could not stop talking about how dangerous it was to go to China and what a pity it would be if they were all killed or died of diseases. Others lauded their actions as heroic acts of Christian service.

Wilfred was not sure what he thought of it all, but when he read the poster, he decided to go and hear the men speak. That night he found himself seated in a packed tent looking up at the Cambridge Seven.

All seven of the young men were introduced to the audience, and then C. T. Studd, the famous cricketer, stood up to speak. His voice was steady as he began.

"About a year ago my brother George was very ill. In fact, the doctor told us there was no hope for him. George and I had played together on the English cricket team against Australia. As I sat by his bedside hour after hour, watching him hover between life and death, thoughts tormented me. I wondered, *Now, what is the popularity of the world worth to George? What can his fame do for him? What is the point of possessing everything the world has to offer, when it's time to face eternity?* And as I wondered, a voice seemed to say to me, 'Vanity, vanity, all is vanity. Only what is done for Christ will last beyond the grave.' Miraculously George did get better, but his illness left me with many questions about my own future."

Although Studd stumbled over some of his words, Wilfred found himself riveted by what he was saying. Having just buried his own father, he had found himself thinking similar thoughts.

Studd went on. "I began to think about my own life. Of course I had attended church for as long as I could remember. I had even heard Moody speak before, but I had never thought about God having a claim on my life. Then one day I felt challenged to yield my whole life to Christ. I knelt down right where I was and asked God to take my life. I promised I would trust in Him and He could direct me to do whatever He wanted. From that time my life has been different. He has given me that peace that passes understanding and a joy unspeakable."

Studd talked on some more, but Wilfred had heard enough. He wanted the same kind of faith that the cricket hero in front of him possessed. *This time,* Wilfred promised himself, *I will not leave the Moody meeting until I find it.*

As the meeting drew to an end, however, Wilfred found it surprisingly difficult to follow through on that promise. Studd called for those who wanted to profess their belief in Christ to stand up. Suddenly Wilfred felt like he was stuck to his seat. He could not will himself to stand up in a crowd of a thousand strangers. Then, in front of him, a teenage boy in a sailor's uniform rose to his feet. Wilfred admired the boy's courage, knowing that for taking such a stand he would be teased by his fellow sailors. But this admiration was soon followed by shame as Wilfred realized how much he was influenced by what strangers thought of him. He would quite happily plunge into icy water or scale a cliff, but he was acting like a coward when it came to Christ. With his heart beating wildly, Wilfred finally managed to clamber to his feet.

There, it's done, he told himself. Like the Cambridge Seven in front of him, Wilfred Grenfell would follow wherever Christ led him. He just did not have the slightest idea where that might be.

Chapter 4

Something Quite Different

At the start of Wilfred's fifth semester in medical school, in February 1885, his mother was still in London working out the last of her husband's affairs before moving back to Parkgate to live with Algernon. It was to her that Wilfred turned for advice.

"I would like to do something to serve Christ, but I don't know what that could be. Do you have any ideas for me?" he asked.

His mother poured two cups of tea and sat down on the leather sofa beside him.

"The church is always a good place to begin. Why don't you ask the Reverend Barraclough at St. Jude's if there is something you could do there?"

Wilfred thought this was a good idea, and so on his next day off he went to visit the Anglican vicar.

He came away with a new title: Sunday-school teacher for junior boys.

This started out as a simple enough task, preparing a Bible lesson to share with the boys on Sunday mornings and leading them in several songs. But it was not long before Wilfred doubted he was having much effect on the nine- and ten-year-old boys. Somehow he just didn't seem to be connecting with them. They were polite enough. Most of them came from respectable, middle-class families, but Wilfred could not find a way to get them excited about the Christian faith. Obviously, he concluded, they were bored, and bored boys do not listen well. Then Wilfred struck on an idea. What if he took the boys out of the church setting and taught them some sporting skills? That way he could get to know them better and find opportunities to share his faith with them along the way.

At the time Wilfred was sharing a house with four other medical students, none of whom had any real use for the living room. Wilfred got permission from them to turn the living room into a gymnasium. He bought wooden poles from a carpenter and constructed parallel bars, and someone gave him two mattresses, which he positioned under the bars. When everything was ready, Wilfred announced that all of the Sunday-school boys and their friends were welcome to come to "sports night," which would be held at his house every Saturday evening. Wilfred promised to teach them boxing, bodybuilding, and gymnastics.

The first Saturday twenty boys were in attendance, and by the end of March, fifty boys were crammed into the house, all eager to learn from Wilfred. He started and ended each session with a Bible reading and prayer, convinced that the boys paid much more attention to the reading than they did to anything he said at Sunday school.

Things were going well until the Reverend Barraclough called Wilfred aside after church one Sunday morning.

"I hear you have a sports club going on Saturday nights," the vicar said sternly.

"Yes, and it's going well," Wilfred replied.

"And what sports are you teaching the lads?"

"I don't have as much room as I would like," Wilfred said, "so I have to confine it to boxing and gymnastics for now. However, if you hear of a bigger facility..." His voice trailed off as he noticed the scowl on the vicar's face.

"That won't be necessary," the vicar snapped. "I asked you to take a simple Sunday-school class, not to teach hordes of boys brutal sports like boxing. You will have to stop the lessons immediately."

Wilfred felt the force of the words as sharply as any well-placed boxing punch. It sent his mind reeling, and it took him a minute to think of an answer. "But when the boys are at my house, I read the Bible to them and find natural ways to talk about my faith. And there is nothing brutal about boxing. Everyone plays by the rules, and it builds strong muscles, and the boys can use it to defend themselves. Why don't you come by this Saturday night and see for yourself?"

The Reverend Barraclough's eyes grew wide. "Mr. Grenfell, I thought I made myself quite clear. I have no intention of visiting your gymnasium. You are to stop these Saturday night activities, or I will have to ask for your resignation."

"Then you have it," Wilfred snapped as he turned and walked out the door.

Wilfred was still stunned by the turn of events when he arrived back at his house. He poured out his problems to one of his housemates, an Australian named Arthur Bobardt. Like Wilfred, Arthur was a Christian, though he had gone about the task of sharing his faith in a different way. He took his Bible and a small harmonium with him each Saturday night and sang and preached in the most dismal areas of London's East End.

"Why don't you join me?" Arthur asked.

Now that his Saturday sports nights had been banned, Wilfred was free, and he agreed to go along.

The experience was more exhilarating than Wilfred could have imagined. He and Arthur ventured into the roughest public houses, where they were spat on and yelled at. Occasionally some drunk would take a swing at one of them, and Wilfred's boxing skills would come in handy. They preached on street corners and sat in the gutters, talking to dejected chimney sweeps and flower sellers about how Jesus Christ could change their lives.

Soon the two of them felt they had to do more than talk, so they started a club for boys on Ratcliff

Highway. The club was a great success from the start, though it did have its problems, of course. Some of the boys stole anything that was not anchored down, and they soon learned to forge Wilfred's signature and write IOUs to the local shops using it. But such behavior only reinforced to Wilfred that these boys needed Christian men as role models. Before long both Arthur and Wilfred had gained their respect, and one by one the boys responded to the gospel.

When he wasn't with the boys, Wilfred worked hard at medical school. Now that he was a Christian, he did not feel right about bribing the record keeper to mark him present when he was not. Nor did he feel good about using crammers to get him through the exams. Instead Wilfred decided to learn all he could, and he started attending all of his lectures and practical assignments. This pleased his adviser, Dr. Treves, and the two of them became good friends.

As summer vacation approached, Wilfred began to think about how much some of the boys in the club would enjoy the rigorous life he led during the summer, wading in the estuary and sailing on the bay. He wished he could climb along the wild rocky coast with the boys and introduce them to the taste of freshly caught shrimp and the smell of the salt marshes.

The more Wilfred thought about it, the fewer reasons he could come up with not to take a dozen or so of the boys back to Parkgate with him for the summer. He began urging the boys to save their pennies, and he promised that if they did so, he would take them on a camping trip they would never forget.

That summer Wilfred brought thirteen boys back to Parkgate with him. They crossed the bay and set up camp on the Welsh coast, where they slept in tents. Wilfred required all the boys to take a bath in the ocean every morning before breakfast. He also taught them to swim, and when he was satisfied their swimming skills were good enough, he took them fishing out on the bay, where they caught their dinner. The boys and Wilfred had a wonderful time together, but before long it was time to head back to London, where in the fall of 1885 Wilfred began his last semester at medical school.

He had no sooner arrived back in London than the Reverend William Davies, the new vicar at St. Jude's, paid him a visit.

"I have heard about the work you did with the boys in the parish," he began, "and I must say, I am very impressed. It is difficult to keep young minds occupied. They are, after all, attached to young bodies. It sounds to me as if you found a good balance."

"Thank you," Wilfred replied, not sure where the conversation was heading.

"I suppose you are wondering why I have come to see you. It's simple, really. We are starting a new club at church. It's for boys, a kind of brigade, and I was wondering if you would consider running it."

"Tell me more about it," Wilfred said cautiously.

"It's up to you how it develops. We just need something to keep the lads occupied and teach them a thing or two in a Christian environment. Just about what you were trying to do with your sports club, I imagine."

"I suppose you know I did run into some, um... problems with the last vicar," Wilfred said.

"Of course, we each have our own way of doing things. I am sure he meant well, but from my point of view, a boys' club is sorely needed."

"I'll try then," Wilfred said. Since leaving the church, he had often wondered what had happened to the boys, and he was glad for the chance to see them again.

This time a proper club was set up, with Dr. Treves as the president, Wilfred as the vice president, and his friend Henry Richards as the secretary. Everything went well from the start, and many boys, both from inside and from outside the church, joined.

In February 1886 Wilfred passed his final exam and was entered as a Member of the Royal College of Physicians and a Member of the Royal College of Surgeons. At twenty-one years of age he was entitled to call himself Dr. Wilfred Grenfell, M.D. His mother and Algernon traveled to London for his graduation ceremony. Wilfred's only regret was that his father was not there to see him graduate.

Now that he was a doctor, Wilfred was offered a position as a house surgeon at London Hospital, under the guidance of Dr. Treves. He accepted the position, and his duties at the hospital and his ongoing involvement with the boys' club kept him busy.

In the middle of 1887, however, Wilfred quit the job of house surgeon and took another group of excited boys from London back to Parkgate for a summer vacation. At the same time, Wilfred was making plans to fulfill a longtime dream. At the end of the summer, he set out for Oxford to study at Queen's College. There he excelled in sports, earning a Rugby Blue, an honor conferred on those who demonstrated great skill in the sport. But while he excelled at rugby and other sports in Oxford, Wilfred found the lifestyle there unsatisfying. So after one semester at Queen's College, he decided to leave the university.

The question for Wilfred soon became what to do next. He knew he could go back to London and work among the poor in the East End, or get a job as a physician in some country area. But none of the positions he heard about appealed to him. Somehow he was sure God had something quite different for him to do; something that no one had ever done before awaited him. If only he could find out what it was.

Chapter 5

On the North Sea

"Sit down, Wilfred. I have something I want to discuss with you," Dr. Treves said.

Wilfred obediently sat himself down in an overstuffed leather chair in the doctor's office.

"I have something exciting to talk with you about, something I think might be just your cup of tea. You are familiar with the deep-sea fishing fleets in the North Sea?"

Wilfred nodded. "Yes, I've treated quite a few fishermen from the North Sea fleets at the hospital. Mainly broken bones and septic gashes. Some of the men were in bad shape because of the length of time it took to get them to the hospital. The longest I recall was fifteen days; we had to amputate his leg."

"Precisely what I want to talk to you about," Dr. Treves continued, leaning forward in his chair. "Six years ago a Mr. Ebenezer Mather was approached by the owner of a fishing fleet and asked to do missionary work among the fishermen on the North Sea fleets. There's up to twenty thousand of them on the water at one time, you know, and the dreaded coper ships from Holland and Belgium are sailing out to them and selling them liquor and tobacco. The tobacco's not so bad, but a trawler on the high sea is no place for a drunken sailor. There's been no end of trouble with brawls and lost working time. Some of the fishermen have even swapped their fishing gear for grog and then told the boat owners that their gear was lost in a storm. It's a bad situation all around."

"It sounds so," Wilfred replied. "Did Mr. Mather ever get the mission work going?"

"Yes. He called it the National Mission to Deep-Sea Fishermen and raised enough money to buy a small smack called the *Ensign*. It goes out among the trawlers, and the men on board give Bible readings and talk to the fishermen about the gospel. It's had some effect, and they have even convinced a few of the owners to declare Sunday a no-fishing day. The boats that stopped fishing on Sundays brought in bigger weekly tallies than those that worked seven days a week."

"Wonderful," Wilfred responded. "That's the kind of work I'd love to do." He watched as Dr. Treves raised his eyebrows.

"I thought that's what you might say," the doctor said. "As a matter of fact, the mission has decided to expand its work on a trial basis. They want to put a doctor on board a boat so that medical work can be carried out on the spot. Many lives could be saved that way, and the mission boats would be an even more welcome sight among the trawlers. What do you think? Are you up for the challenge?"

Wilfred laughed. "Up for the challenge! When do I start?"

Dr. Treves also laughed. "A new ship, the *Thomas Grey*, sails out of Gorleston in early January. Being out on the North Sea in the dead of winter should test your mettle. You'll soon know whether this is the life for you. Shall I tell them you'll be there?"

"Absolutely," Wilfred replied. "This is just what I've been waiting for."

After working nine months as a house surgeon at London Hospital and waiting for the right opportunity to come along, Wilfred was eager to get started on this new challenge. In the following weeks, he wound up his affairs in London and handed over the responsibility for the boys' club to another young Christian student, who was happy to take on the job. Then he returned to Parkgate for Christmas. Finally, on January 1, 1888, he set out for London by train. At Liverpool Street Station he transferred to the train to Yarmouth, located on the east coast of England.

It was early evening when the train reached Yarmouth. A steady rain had set in, and wind whipped around Wilfred as he stepped onto the station platform. A sailor dressed in an oilskin raincoat was waiting to greet him and escort him to the ship docked at nearby Gorleston. When they reached the harbor, Wilfred scanned the horizon for the *Thomas Grey*, but he could see no boat big enough.

"Where is the boat docked?" he asked the sailor accompanying him.

"Down there," the sailor replied, pointing to the top of the masts rising above the dock. "It's a particularly low tide tonight."

Surprised, Wilfred walked to the edge of the dock and looked down. There was the *Thomas Grey*. He let out a gasp. He had been expecting a large ship, but the *Thomas Grey* was not much bigger than the fishing trawler he and Algernon had sailed around on the River Dee estuary. It looked barely big enough to survive the turbulent waters of the North Sea.

Wilfred threw his bag down onto the deck of the boat and then slid down a yardarm after it. It wasn't until he was standing on the deck that he realized that the yardarm had just been greased and tarred in preparation for putting to sea, and now his suit was smeared with grease and tar.

Once Wilfred was on board, the captain introduced himself to him and showed him to his small cabin below deck. Wilfred slept soundly in his new quarters, and the following morning the *Thomas Grey* put to sea.

The first port of call was Ostend, Belgium, where the captain would buy duty-free goods to sell to the fishermen for a small profit. Even getting that far was a test of Wilfred's commitment to his new call in life. It was bitter cold, one of the coldest winters in years, and Wilfred soon discovered that sailing on the open ocean in the middle of winter was much different from puttering around in a boat on the water off Parkgate in summer.

Much to Wilfred's surprise, one day into the voyage he got seasick. His stomach churned with every rise and fall of the boat. The only heat in his cabin was from a small oil stove whose strong fumes added to his misery. He soon turned the stove off, and the second morning he awoke to find that icicles had formed on the deck head above him. Determined not to be beaten by seasickness, Wilfred decided that what he needed was physical exercise. He dragged himself up on deck and forced his body to run around the perimeter of the deck.

It was a difficult feat, since the little boat was pitching and rolling and the deck was constantly doused with seawater that turned to ice. But after half an hour of this activity, Wilfred began to feel a little better. He stayed up on deck talking to the captain about navigation until lunchtime.

The boat reached Ostend in two and a half days, and Wilfred was glad to see land again. He wrote home to his mother, "I wish I were a better sailor, and hope this trip will make me one, as it will be impossible to doctor others if I am ill myself."

Wilfred had never been outside the United Kingdom before, and he looked forward to meeting some Flemish people. As soon as the *Thomas Grey* docked in Ostend, he went ashore and made friends. Soon he was skating along the frozen rivers and canals with them.

The weather continued to grow colder, and by the time four tons of supplies had been loaded into the little ship's hold, the vessel was stuck firmly in the ice. A steamship, which was also heading out to sea, obligingly churned up the ice enough for the captain of the *Thomas Grey* to cast off and maneuver into the deep channel that led to the open sea. If everything went well, they would see land again in eight weeks.

Much to Wilfred's relief the seasickness left him, which was a good thing because he was headed into some of the world's roughest water. The North Sea was actually a very shallow stretch of water, at times a barely submerged bridge between England and the European continent. Because it was so shallow, the water whipped up into huge waves at the first sign of a storm.

Every morning, impervious to the cold, Wilfred stripped naked and took a snow bath on the deck of the ship. His shipmates could hardly believe anyone would volunteer to do this, but Wilfred explained that it was good for the circulation. After lunch he practiced gymnastics on the foredeck, much to the continued amazement of his shipmates.

Five days out of Ostend the captain yelled, "Fleet ahead." Wilfred stared out across the waves. Sure enough, to starboard he could make out the shape of a smack rising and falling in the churning ocean, and then he saw another and another. Each of them was flying the fleet's green-and-red flag.

"Will we go aboard?" Wilfred asked the captain.

"Not while they have their nets down, Doctor," the captain replied. "Even the most pious captain would not welcome us at that moment. No, we will fall into formation with them, put our own nets over the side, and do a little fishing ourselves. When the nets are all hauled in and the fish stowed away, then it will be visiting time."

Wilfred helped as the *Thomas Grey*'s nets were lowered over the stern of the vessel. Once the net was overboard, the captain ordered the sails hoisted, and the ship began to trawl for cod.

When the "admiral," the man who coordinated the actions of the fishing fleet, fired off a flare, it was time to start hauling in the nets. This was hard, backbreaking work, and Wilfred pitched in to help the crew. Slowly the net began to emerge from the frigid, gray water of the North Sea until only the cod end, the end of the net where the fish were trapped, was still in the water. Wire ropes were then put through the net, and the cod end was hoisted up and swung over the deck. One of the crewmen agilely undid the knot that held the cod end closed, and the catch of cod spilled out onto the deck. Now it was time to gut and process the fish to get them ready to take to market. This was a messy and dangerous undertaking, as fishermen wielded razor-sharp knives while they were jostled back and forth by the ocean. Again Wilfred willingly got to work, eager to learn as much as he could about fishing in the North Sea.

Eventually all the cod were processed and ready to be transported to market by carrier boats that serviced the fishing fleet. The money raised selling the fish that the crew of the *Thomas Grey* had caught went toward helping to finance the work of the National Mission to Deep-Sea Fishermen.

It wasn't long after the nets had been hauled aboard the *Thomas Grey* that the first patient arrived for Wilfred to treat. He was a twelve-year-old boy with a fishhook stuck in his hand. He was ferried to the *Thomas Grey* in a small dinghy that pitched and rolled and beat against the side of the ship as the boy climbed precariously up a rope ladder using only one hand.

Wilfred carefully removed the large hook that was embedded deep in the palm of the boy's right hand. Once he had removed the hook, he dressed the wound and wrapped a thick bandage around it. When he learned that the boy had no hat to keep his ears warm against the biting winter wind, Wilfred quickly found him one from a supply kept aboard the *Thomas Grey* for such situations. Soon the boy was on his way back to his trawler, his hand bandaged tightly and a warm new woolen cap pulled down over his ears.

Two more men were ferried to the *Thomas Grey*. They were both in their twenties. One had been injured when a boom had broken loose, and the other had infected sores on the back of his neck where his oilskin raincoat had rubbed the skin bare. Not only did the first man have a nasty gash on the side of his face from his encounter with the boom but also his left arm was broken, and as Wilfred examined him further, he discovered that two of his ribs had been crushed. Wilfred set to work, first setting the man's broken arm and then attending to the gash. Finally he wound a bandage around the man's midsection to strap his fractured ribs.

Then it was on to the next patient. This man's ailment was common among the nearly twenty thousand fishermen who served on some three hundred fishing trawlers and smacks on the North Sea. The fishermen believed that it brought them bad luck if they bathed while they were at sea. They lived in the same set of clothes, which were often damp, for up to three months at a time. The damp clothing and the oilskin wet-weather gear the men wore often caused chafing, which, if left unattended in the unsanitary conditions aboard most of the boats, soon turned septic. Since Wilfred was the only doctor among the fishing fleet, he soon found much of his time taken up dressing such wounds.

By the time he arrived back in Gorleston, Wilfred Grenfell was convinced of one thing—working among fishermen was to be his life's work. He signed on for another trip out to the fishing fleet, and by Christmas 1888 he was a valued member of the National Mission to Deep-Sea Fishermen. Indeed, he was so valuable that Ebenezer Mather offered him a permanent position and a salary of three hundred pounds a year. Wilfred eagerly accepted the offer.

Within a year Wilfred had been promoted all the way up to superintendent of the mission and was in charge of all the activities at Gorleston as ships and crews came and went from there. This new responsibility meant that he had to live permanently in Gorleston, where he found lodging with William Cockrill, a prominent architect who had built a spacious home on a bluff overlooking the River Yare and the North Sea.

One day, as he sat looking out the picture window of his new sitting room, Wilfred had to admit that as beautiful as his surroundings and the view were, he would still rather be at sea. Being holed up in a pokey cold cabin while the ship pitched and rolled with the tide was much more exciting to him than being stuck on land most of the time, as Wilfred now was taking care of administration. Yet he knew that this was where he could do the most good at the present time.

Wilfred could not give up his ties with the ocean entirely. Every morning, winter or summer, he climbed down the bluff to the sea below and leaped into the surf for an invigorating swim. He built a small canvas canoe, which he named *Tip-Me-Not*, and on the most storm-swept days, he launched her and paddled far out into the ocean.

Alcohol was one of the biggest enemies that affected the lives of the fishermen. When the men came ashore, they collected their pay and went straight to the public houses, where they quickly drank away their wages, often leaving their wives and children without enough food or clothing. Wilfred decided to do something about this situation. When an old seamen's hall in Gorleston came available, the National Mission to Deep-Sea Fishermen took over the facility and set up a club for fishermen. The club was a great success, and soon the building was brimming with fishermen who came to play games, read, and talk to people about their faith in an environment where there was no alcohol.

Wilfred's personality, which drew so many fishermen to the club, was also a great asset in fundraising. Keeping a ministry like the National Mission to Deep-Sea Fishermen running required a lot of money, and along with his other responsibilities, Wilfred traveled the country talking in churches and at living-room meetings about the work of the mission and asking people to support it. Wilfred's homespun way of speaking was both exciting and engaging as he told stories of the practical ways the mission was attempting to share the gospel message among the fishermen of the North Sea. His approach won people over, and they willingly stepped forward to support the mission. Wilfred was gratified with the generosity of such people, and he looked forward to new challenges that the National Mission to Deep-Sea Fishermen could take on.

Chapter 6

Labrador

"Have you seen this month's issue of *Toilers of the Sea* yet?" William Cockrill asked Wilfred.

Toilers of the Sea was the official magazine of the National Mission to Deep-Sea Fishermen, and Wilfred had not yet seen the latest edition. "No," he replied, "I've been down at the boathouse all day. Does it have a good article in it?"

"Good article!" William exclaimed. "This one will rock England, if I'm not mistaken. It's about the pitiful conditions along the Labrador coast. Hard to believe that there are people in a British colony leading such desperate lives. Here, take a look."

Wilfred leaned over and took the magazine, which was open to an article by Francis Hopwood. He began to read. Hopwood had recently visited the Labrador coast, and he described in detail the deplorable conditions he had encountered under which the people there were living.

When he had finished reading, Wilfred let out a whistle. "I agree with you. This is going to stir things up. The Church of England minister in St. John's has been writing to the mission for years, asking for help, but we haven't had the funds to get over there. God willing, Hopwood's article might change all of that. The people certainly sound in a bad way."

Over the next two weeks, the article did stir up a great deal of interest, not only in Great Britain but also in Canada and the United States. It was reprinted in every important newspaper in these countries, and a public cry of protest went up for the fishermen who worked under such deplorable conditions. Money began to flow into the National Mission to Deep-Sea Fishermen, earmarked for work among the Labrador "fisherfolk."

This cry to do something was amplified in early 1892, when news arrived in England that forty of the two hundred fishermen working out of Trinity Bay in eastern Newfoundland had perished. The men had gone out to fish before all the ice had thawed in the bay and had been caught in a blizzard. Their fishing boats were crushed in the ice, and the men were left to freeze to death. Far out to sea other fishermen found the haunting remains of crushed boats, their crews, frozen solid, clinging to them.

Once again public sympathy was aroused. The Lord Mayor of London opened a fund for the families of the frozen men, and Queen Victoria contributed and sent a personal message to the widows and children.

Everyone in the mission agreed that something had to be done. The money and the public interest were there. It was time for the men to take an exploratory voyage to see how they could help. Without a moment's hesitation, Wilfred volunteered for the voyage. The vote to accept him as leader of the expedition was unanimous, and a month after news of the disaster among the fishermen broke in England, Wilfred found himself preparing one of the mission's ships, the *Albert*, for his longest voyage yet.

Wilfred attacked his new assignment with gusto, helping the mission's carpenters to sheath the hull of the *Albert* in an extra layer of timber and reinforce her bow so that she could plow her way through ice. The area below deck was remodeled so that partitions could be slid aside, allowing up to one hundred people to attend Christian services on board. In another area of the vessel, nursing bunks, an operating room, and a dispensary were installed. Since the hatches were too small to pass through a man on a stretcher, they were enlarged and fitted with metal hatch covers.

As Wilfred wrote reports of his preparations in *Toilers of the Sea,* donations began to flow in for the people of Labrador. There were bales of used clothing from church drives in Cornwall, books schoolchildren had collected in Scotland, and medical supplies from Sunday schools in Wales. When it was time to depart, there was so much cargo on board that one of the mission helpers jokingly complained to Wilfred, "She's loaded to the gunwales, and that's because she has so much reading in her, and it ain't light reading, neither."

The mission committee decided that June was the best time of year to begin the voyage, and on June 12 Wilfred proudly boarded the *Albert*. He, like the rest of the crew, was dressed in serge trousers and a blue jersey with the name of the mission embroidered in gold lettering on the chest.

The *Albert* was towed out of the River Yare. At 110 feet long, she was the biggest vessel in the mission's growing fleet, and Wilfred was confident that her newly reinforced oak and teak hull could take the pounding of the wild Atlantic Ocean. The town's pier was crowded with people as the ship departed, and others spilled out along the river's edge as the *Albert* was towed by. Wilfred could make out the faces of many fishermen, their wives, and their children. He knew their lives were better now because of the work of the National Mission to Deep-Sea Fishermen, and he prayed that he would find a way to help the fishermen of Labrador and Newfoundland as well.

Once the ship was across the bar and into the open ocean, Captain Trezisse yelled his orders. "Man the rigging. Hoist the square sail."

Wilfred leaped into action. It felt so good to be on board a ship again.

The plan was to sail nonstop to Newfoundland, but the weather proved to be their enemy. From the start the *Albert* faced fog and strong headwinds, and three days out she sprang a leak, taking on thirty inches of water a day.

The captain called Wilfred into his cabin. "I think we need to beach her and find that leak," he said, shaking his head. "It's manageable at the moment, but we can't take a chance in the Atlantic. I'm changing course to head for Crookhaven, Ireland."

"Quite right," Wilfred agreed, although he was disappointed. He had wanted to see how quickly they could make the run across the Atlantic Ocean, and here they were, meeting delays within days of leaving Yarmouth.

Still, Wilfred made the most of it. These were coastal people, and many of them read *Toilers of the Sea* and were familiar with Wilfred's mission. They flocked to see the *Albert,* now beached in shallow water, and to get medical advice and supplies from Wilfred, who happily obliged and was paid for his effort in eggs and vegetables for the voyage.

On July 3 Captain Trezisse announced that he had been unable to find the leak and he hoped it had sealed itself. They needed to be on their way, and so on the high tide, the *Albert* was towed to deeper water, and she sailed from Crookhaven the following day.

Much to everyone's relief, the ship did not take on any more water. The head winds were strong, and a thick fog persisted until they were over a thousand miles out into the Atlantic. Still, despite the weather conditions, the ship managed to cover about 130 miles a day. Then, unexpectedly, the winds died, leaving the *Albert* to limp along, taking advantage of every puff of wind that came her way.

Wilfred and the rest of the crew busied themselves keeping everything shipshape. They painted and polished for hours each morning, and in the afternoons Wilfred held a Bible study. The carpenter was a cornet player, and he accompanied the crew as they sang hymns on deck.

Finally, on the morning of July 21, the captain announced that, according to his calculations, they should be nearing St. John's, and he sent a watch up to the crow's nest. Around lunchtime the welcome words "Land ahoy!" reverberated around the ship. Wilfred took out his spyglass and aimed it westward. He looked through it and stared in disbelief. There was land ahead all right, but there was something else as well. Above the rugged coastline, a plume of black smoke rose into the sky.

Wilfred turned to speak to Captain Trezisse, who was also viewing the scene through a spyglass.

"What do you make of it?" he asked.

Captain Trezisse shook his head. "Grim news for the people of St. John's," he replied. "There's so much smoke, the whole town must be ablaze."

"So it is St. John's that is burning?"

"Without a doubt," the captain said.

As the *Albert* inched closer to her destination, the scene became clearer. Although the town of St. John's itself was shielded from the Atlantic Ocean by a rocky cliff, Wilfred could soon make out huge plumes of flame shooting into the late afternoon sky. Occasionally tiny cinders landed on the ship, and the captain posted everyone on watch in case a cinder ignited the ship.

No tug came out to guide them into the harbor, so the captain ordered the sails lowered, and the ship dropped anchor outside the port for the night. Wilfred sat on deck all evening watching the reflection of the flames dance eerily on the frigid ocean. He prayed for the people of St. John's and for the work he hoped to do on this rocky coast.

As dawn broke, a tugboat approached the *Albert*. The news from the pilot was grim. He reported that a fire had been started by a young boy carelessly throwing a lighted match into a barn situated on a hill above the town. Fanned by a strong northwest wind, sparks and cinders from the barn fire quickly set the rest of the town afire.

Soon the *Albert* was being towed into St. John's Harbor. As she rounded the headland of the cliff, the crew got their first opportunity to see what the fire had done. Most of the buildings had been reduced to piles of smoking, black embers. Only the stone chimneys of the buildings remained standing, blackened witnesses to the devastation around them.

Amazingly, no one had been killed in the fire, though two thousand buildings had been destroyed, leaving eleven thousand people dazed and homeless. Most of them had escaped with only the clothes on their backs, and Wilfred was grateful for the bails of used clothing stowed away in the *Albert*'s hold. He and the rest of the crew spent the day unpacking and distributing them.

Newfoundland was a self-governing British colony. At about two o'clock in the afternoon, Wilfred looked up from his work to see a procession coming toward him. It consisted of the premier of Newfoundland, Sir William Whiteway, and five members of the colony's government. The colony's governor, Sir Terence O'Brien, was away in England at the time. The delegation had come to welcome the *Albert* and offer any assistance they could to Wilfred and the crew. Wilfred was impressed; even in the midst of their own tragedy, they wanted to help the mission get established along the coast. They even offered to hire a pilot for the trip north, as the rocky outcrops around the coast could easily prove fatal to someone who did not know the waters, especially since the coast was too remote to have lighthouses.

As the days went by, many people, including Dr. Moses Harvey, the Church of England minister in the city, offered advice to Wilfred. There were still three months of the cod-fishing season left, and they suggested that Wilfred go north along the Labrador coast until he found the fleet of one hundred or so fishing schooners. Wilfred and the crew, along with their new pilot, a lively Irishman named Captain Fitzpatrick, were eager to get under way, but fog delayed them until Tuesday, August 2, 1892.

The expedition headed north from St. John's, past the coast of Newfoundland island and across the Strait of Belle Isle, which separated the island from Labrador. A week later Wilfred had his first glimpse of the Labrador coast. The *Albert* emerged from a bank of thick fog into a beautiful, bright, sunny morning. On the horizon Wilfred could see rocky cliffs rising straight up from the sea. Beyond the cliffs, dense vegetation covered hills that climbed slowly to become jagged, snow-covered peaks. Small, rocky, treeless islands jutted from the sea like sentinels guarding the coastline. Between the islands and the ship bobbed icebergs, broken off from glaciers in Greenland and drifting south on the current. They reflected the sun in a shower of radiance. Beneath the *Albert* schools of cod and other fish teemed, roiling the water silver. Whales fed blissfully on these fish, breaking the surface intermittently with a hiss and a spout as they arched up for a breath. Overhead the sky was filled with gulls and other seabirds, some of which Wilfred had never seen before. Wilfred watched as birds threw themselves headlong into the ocean and emerged with squirming fish held firmly in their beaks. The birds headed with their catch for the rocky cliffs, where thousands of nests clung to the nooks and crags. Standing on deck a long time to take in the vista, Wilfred marveled at the sight.

Progress up the Labrador coast was slow because the captain would not sail in darkness. There were too many icebergs and uncharted rocky outcrops to risk doing that. In fact, the maps and charts the captain was using were based on those made by Captain Cook when he visited the area in 1770. Wilfred took this as a challenge, spending many hours taking readings on headlands and coves to add more detail to the aging maps.

Wilfred also made hourly notations on the weather as the *Albert* progressed up the coast. They were sailing in the same latitudes as the British Isles, but the climate was completely different. The ocean currents around the British Isles came from the South Atlantic Ocean, and they created a warm cushion of air around the islands. Labrador's current, on the other hand, swept down from the Arctic Circle to meet a warmer southern current. As the two currents clashed, they produced weather that could go from warm to freezing in less than an hour. Howling winds could whip up in an instant, creating treacherous conditions for fishermen.

On the fourth day, the *Albert* sailed through a channel called Domino Run and into a sheltered harbor, where they dropped anchor for the night. The mission flag was raised, and within minutes boats began to draw alongside, as curious fishermen came aboard to meet the doctor. Many of them told Wilfred they had heard that a mission ship with a doctor aboard was headed their way, but they hardly believed it was true.

Wilfred greeted everyone who came on board and took the visitors on tours below deck. He treated some of the fishermen for stomach ailments and infected cuts. Many of them had never seen a doctor in their lives, and they were eager to see what Wilfred could do for them.

About two hours after they had anchored, Wilfred noticed an unseaworthy boat tie up alongside the *Albert*. In it sat a wizened old man. He stared up at Wilfred for a minute and then yelled, "Be you a real doctor?"

Wilfred nodded and leaned over the gunwale. "Yes, I am," he called down.

"Us hasn't got no money, but there's a sick man ashore. You'd come and see him?"

"I'll get my bag and be right with you," Wilfred said.

Wilfred smiled to himself as he went below to get his medical bag. The old man was a Liveyere, the people who lived along the coast year-round. Most of them were of Irish, Scottish, and Cornish descent, and they had a peculiar way of speaking. Their name for themselves came from being asked where they came from. They replied, "We live here," which got shortened to Liveyeres.

Wilfred did not think twice about getting into the lopsided little boat. If the worst happened and it capsized, he knew he could easily swim to shore.

All went well, and when they reached land, the old man climbed out and summoned Wilfred to follow him up a mossy path that led to a tiny hut with a turf roof and one small window with a piece of broken glass in it. Wilfred had to stoop down to get through the door. Inside, a dank smell greeted him, and it took a moment for his eyes to adjust to the darkness. Rough-hewn bunks lined the walls, and a little cast-iron stove sat in the middle of the room.

Apart from that there was no furniture in the place. Six half-clad, wide-eyed children sat on the pebble floor staring up at Wilfred.

"Hello," he said. "What are your names?"

One by one they mumbled their names, and then the oldest one said, "Be it true? Came you here to doctor our pa?"

Then Wilfred heard the sound of a hacking cough, and he looked closely at the pile of rags on one of the bottom bunks. There was a person in there.

"That be our pa," one of the other children said.

"And where is your mother?" Wilfred asked.

"She be down salting fish. I'm in charge," the oldest boy said.

Wilfred tousled the boy's hair and walked over to his patient. He knelt down beside the man and felt his pulse. It was faint. Then he examined his chest. There was only one diagnosis—a death sentence—tuberculosis.

Wilfred gave the oldest child some medicine to relieve his father's cough and instructed him to come out to the *Albert* in the morning. He promised them clothing and blankets for their father and some fat and flour for cooking. Then he gathered the children around and prayed for them.

He left the hut with a heavy heart. Although what he had just seen matched exactly what Francis Hopwood had described in his article in *Toilers of the Sea*, it was still shocking to see such poverty up close, especially when there was nowhere the people could turn for help. In London the poorest people could line up at the Salvation Army soup kitchens or go to the emergency ward at London Hospital for treatment. But here on the remote Labrador coast, there were no charities, no hospitals, and no schools.

As he was ferried back to the *Albert*, Wilfred wondered about his call to deep-sea fishermen. Yes, of course they needed medical attention and the gospel, but the hopelessness in the eyes of the children he had just visited haunted him. Surely there was something he could do for them as well.

Chapter 7

Back to Labrador

The *Albert* made her way farther up the Labrador coast, alternating between visiting the fishing fleet working the rich fishing ground of the Grand Banks and visiting the small communities dotted along the coastline. Wherever the men were, the people were excited to see them.

As the ship made her way up the coast, Wilfred found variations of the circumstances he had seen at Domino Run. Teenagers had rickets, young men coughed blood, and little girls suffered from exposure from wearing nothing more than two flour sacks sewn together with fishing line. And he met with the same level of surprise. Although news of the presence of the *Albert* spread quickly up the coast, few people believed it would actually stop in their tiny settlement or that there really was a doctor on board who would treat them for free.

The more Wilfred saw of conditions on the Labrador coast, the angrier he became. These fishermen and their families, both the Liveyeres and those who wintered over in St. John's and came north to fish off Labrador in the summer, found themselves in hopeless situations. In talking with Captain Fitzgerald, Wilfred learned that the trawler owners and the fish merchants liked it that way. They preferred to keep the fishermen, particularly the strong young men, in debt to them as a way of keeping them fishing year after year. To do this, they set the price of the catch, no matter how large or small it was, to cover only the bare necessities of life. A Labrador fisherman found himself working nonstop for the five-month fishing season, then subsisting with his family on a few barrels of flour, several quarts of molasses, tea, and fat, all sold to him by the trawler owners at inflated prices.

The fishermen supplemented their diet with any fish they had managed to dry for themselves during the summer, and those who owned rifles and could afford bullets shot small game, such as foxes and deer, to eat. There was no money left over to buy clothing or fishing equipment, and year after year the fishermen and their families sank further and further into debt buying their basic commodities from the trawler owners.

Wilfred met only one missionary working among the Liveyeres, but in Hopedale, the northernmost point of the *Albert*'s voyage up the coast, he did encounter a band of Moravian missionaries. The Moravians, whose predecessors had been coming to Labrador for over a hundred years to work among the Eskimos, welcomed Wilfred and put him straight to work. One of the first patients he saw there was a man whose arms had both been blown off when a cannon misfired. Although the Moravians had done what they could, the stumps of the man's arms had become gangrenous. Wilfred took the man back to the *Albert* and operated to remove the gangrene. It was uncertain whether or not the man would live, but Wilfred knew that without the medical aid he had given, the man would have died an agonizing death.

Other cases were more straightforward to treat and yet rendered dramatic results. A fisherman had hobbled around for three years with what he thought was an incurable foot ailment. It turned out to be nothing more than an ingrown toenail, which Wilfred was able to correct in a matter of minutes. The fisherman was then able to go back to work making a scant living for his family.

In October the fishing boats sailed back to St. John's to avoid being iced in for the winter. By this time Wilfred and the crew of the *Albert* had given away all the clothing, books, and magazines aboard, visited fifty settlements, treated nine hundred patients, and held hundreds of church services on land and sea. Most of Wilfred's patients had never before seen a doctor or a midwife, and they knew very little about medical matters. In the absence of a doctor, many people had invented "cures" for themselves. Some of these cures appalled Wilfred, who wondered how such superstitions could be passed on as medicine along the coast. One old woman he met prescribed swallowing nine lice every third day for nine days as a cure for stomach ailments. Another time he saw an amulet around a man's neck that contained the tooth of a dying deer, a sure way to stop fits, he was told. Perhaps the most common cure that Wilfred saw was a mixture of white paint and herbs, which was supposed to draw out an abscess.

The *Albert* followed the fishing fleet back to St. John's. On the way down the coast, she stopped in once again at Domino Run, where Wilfred had tended his first patient. It was a somber moment when he walked past a freshly dug grave on his way up the mossy trail to the dirt hut. A woman confirmed his worst fears: her husband had died two weeks before. Wilfred's heart broke as he surveyed the scene: six young children and their widowed mother, all looking thin and ill. He offered them some of what was left of the ship's supplies and once again prayed for them before he left.

The *Albert* sailed into St. John's Harbor to a rousing welcome. Many of the fishing boats were already anchored in the harbor, and news of the *Albert*'s service to the fishermen and residents of Labrador had spread throughout the town. Willing hands reached out to take the *Albert*'s mooring lines as she tied up alongside the wharf, and many people offered food and housing to the crew. Wilfred was invited to stay with Governor Sir Terence O'Brien, who had returned from England. As Wilfred accompanied the governor to his house, he was amazed to see the progress that had been made in rebuilding the town. Many new wooden houses and warehouses dotted the rocky inlet.

Everywhere Wilfred went, fishermen and their families flocked around him, thanking him for his service and the encouraging work he was doing.

Within hours of arriving back in St. John's, it seemed that every door in the place was open to the National Mission to Deep-Sea Fishermen. A reporter from the local newspaper interviewed Wilfred for a lead article on the work of the mission. A committee of politicians and merchants invited Wilfred to address them on the needs he had seen on his trip and to offer suggestions on how to meet those needs. Wilfred and Captain Trezisse attended the meeting together, and they were excited to see how serious those in attendance were about tackling the problems fishermen faced. At the meeting Dr. Moses Harvey proposed a resolution thanking the National Mission to Deep-Sea Fishermen and their missionaries. Then he added, "This meeting also desires to express the hope that the directors of the mission may see their way to continue the work thus begun, and should they do so, they may be assured of the warmest support and cooperation of all classes in this community."

Another meeting followed the first, and Wilfred was delighted to see just how much help the politicians and merchants of St. John's were willing to give. The government offered to erect two hospitals, leaving the sites for them up to the mission to decide. They also offered to furnish the hospitals according to the directions submitted by the mission's hospital committee and to pay for the maintenance and upkeep of the buildings. A prominent merchant, Baine Grieve, offered a large house in Battle Harbor, on the south coast of Labrador, to be used as one of the hospitals. Wilfred thought the second hospital should be situated at Indian Harbor at the mouth of Hamilton Inlet, midway up the coast.

While these developments excited Wilfred, in his mind they were only the beginning. The *Albert* was a sturdy vessel, but she was dependent on the right wind conditions for power. Wilfred thought that a steam-powered launch would be a much more versatile craft in a variety of weather conditions. He envisioned doctors and nurses manning the hospitals while he steamed up and down the coast, stopping in on the Liveyeres and tending to the immediate needs of the fishing fleet.

Finally, after the meetings were over and the ship was restocked, it was time to set out across the Atlantic for England. On November 8 half of the population of St. John's turned out to see the *Albert* off. As Wilfred waved from the bow he yelled to the people, "I promise we'll be back. God bless you all till we meet again."

Soon they were out in the open water of the Atlantic Ocean. The waves were high, but by now the crew of the *Albert* worked seamlessly together, and they encountered only one problem on the twelve-day passage to England. On day six of the voyage, when all of the maintenance work was completed for the day, Wilfred started a game of cricket on deck with several other crew members. By now they were down to only one cricket ball, the others having been batted overboard during previous games.

About ten minutes into the game, Wilfred watched in dismay as the last ball sailed past him and splashed into the ocean. He looked down at it bobbing on the surface. There would be no more cricket games on board during the voyage. In an instant Wilfred kicked off his shoes and yelled over his shoulder, "Tell the captain to tack back and pick me up." With that he climbed over the railing and dived into the water. The sudden cold of the ocean took his breath away, but he surfaced and began swimming toward the ball. As he did so, he watched the *Albert* tacking away from him!

Wilfred recovered the ball and stuck it in his pocket, but it was another twenty minutes before the ship tacked back and came alongside him. He treaded water and waited patiently for it to arrive. When the *Albert* had finally maneuvered close enough to him, he grabbed the rope ladder that dangled over the side and climbed back aboard. Once he was safely on deck, Wilfred learned that the captain had been so shocked when he dived overboard that he had tacked in the wrong direction. Wilfred laughed at the mistake. Treading icy cold water was just the kind of challenge he loved. He went below and changed his clothes, and then the cricket game continued.

The remaining six days of the voyage were uneventful, and soon the ship was docking in Yarmouth. Everyone, including the mission council, was eager to hear about the crew's experiences in Newfoundland. Within days of arriving back in England, Wilfred was off to London to give a report to the council. He told the gathered council members about all he had seen and the small ways they had been able to help the people of Labrador on both land and sea. He painted a picture for them of what could be done with more medical missionaries and resources.

In return the council filled Wilfred in on what had been happening in the mission during the six months he had been away. They now had eleven ships and had extended their ministry to fishermen on the south and west coasts of England and to Ireland. Obviously, they explained, the mission had spread out, and they were not sure whether there was enough momentum to fund a work overseas. The voyage of the *Albert* had cost two thousand pounds, and they could not commit to spending that amount on a regular basis.

Such talk only served to challenge Wilfred, who set out with Captain Trezisse on a speaking tour of England to raise money for mission work on the

Labrador coast. Everywhere he went, Wilfred captivated audiences, and the money flowed in. Many local committees were formed, each one undertaking to sponsor one bed in the new hospitals the committee in St. John's had promised to provide. When Wilfred spoke to the boys at Mostyn House School in Parkgate, they enthusiastically offered to sponsor a bed as well. When he told the boys the story of playing cricket on the *Albert*'s deck and losing the ball overboard, one of them suggested Wilfred drill a hole through the ball and tether it to the ship's railing. Wilfred thought this was an interesting idea and promised to report back on how well it worked.

Based on Wilfred's success in fundraising, the board of the National Mission to Deep-Sea Fishermen voted in February 1893 to continue and extend the work in Labrador, with Wilfred heading it up. Nothing could have delighted Wilfred more. He longed to be back among the Liveyeres and the fishermen, bringing them the message of hope and healing their bodies.

It was a warm day in May when the *Albert* was once again towed out of the River Yare. On board were three doctors: Wilfred Grenfell, Eliot Curwen, and Wilfred's old friend, the Australian, Arthur Bobardt. Two nurses, Celia Williams and Ada Carwardine, would soon set sail for St. John's aboard an Allen Line steamer.

Wilfred grinned from ear to ear as he watched the commotion around him. The fishermen's brass band played energetically on the *Albert*'s deck, the other mission ships in port were rigged with fluttering flags, and the sound of the cheering crowd was punctuated with signal guns saluting the crew and their mission. In the ship's hold, thousands of pounds of donated goods—clothing, books, and supplies to equip the hospitals—were packed away in bales.

As the *Albert* was towed out into the open ocean, Wilfred watched the crowd slowly fade into the distance. The brass band and other visitors who had been aboard transferred to the tugboat, and then the towline was let go. Once again they were on their way. This time, though, they planned to stop at many ports along the south coast of England, where Wilfred and Captain Trezisse intended to speak at as many churches and halls as possible. As they informed people about their proposed work in Labrador, Wilfred prayed that somehow God would provide them with the steam launch they desperately needed to work between the two hospitals.

About halfway through their coastal tour, Wilfred's prayer was answered. The London office sent the wonderful news that money had been given to buy a steam launch. And Wilfred knew exactly where to find one. He had seen a forty-five-foot river launch in Chester that he had admired when he was visiting his brother Algernon nearby in Parkgate. The vessel was for sale for 250 pounds, less than half the cost of building her. The *Albert* continued on the tour without Wilfred, who headed north by land to see if the launch was still for sale. Thankfully it was, and he bought it on the spot.

Algernon helped him to quickly outfit it for ocean work, and then Wilfred convinced the Allen Line to carry the small craft to St. John's aboard one of its large steamships at a bargain price.

By the time the *Princess May*, as the launch was called, was finally stowed in the hold of an Allen Line ship, the *Albert* was in Queenstown, Ireland. Wilfred rejoined the vessel there, and they headed out across the Atlantic Ocean on June 7, 1893.

Wilfred spent his time reading medical texts, conducting Bible studies, and learning more about navigation from Captain Trezisse. He was interested to learn that they were taking a more northerly route to St. John's this time, a route called the Great Circle course. About halfway through the voyage, the *Albert* was surrounded by towering icebergs. Soon fog engulfed the ship, and it was all hands on deck to watch out for the looming white shapes that could rip the hull open and sink the ship.

Thanks to Captain Trezisse's skill, the *Albert* reached the safety of St. John's Harbor on June 26. As the *Albert* was towed in through the narrow, rock-walled channel to the harbor, the people of St. John's gathered to welcome the vessel back. Wilfred and the crew disembarked to huge cheers and an invitation to dine with the governor that night.

Over the next few days, Wilfred spoke at every church in town. He was thrilled to learn that the committee had gone ahead with plans to outfit two hospitals, and the local community had collected fifteen hundred dollars for the mission to spend helping fishermen. The Allen Line steamer also arrived, bringing with it the two nurses and the *Princess May*. The nurses were welcomed with open arms, as they were the only two registered nurses in Newfoundland. The local people begged them to stay and work in St. John's, but Wilfred was determined that they should serve those who had for so long been beyond the reach of medical help. He promised to recruit more nurses to be stationed in St. John's.

When the *Princess May* was slung out of the cargo hold and into the water, her funnel was missing and her propeller shaft was bent. No one was sure what had happened to the launch, and Wilfred had to wait while a new funnel was made and the shaft was straightened.

Finally, on July 6, the *Princess May* was christened and commissioned for her work along the Labrador coast. With that formality over, Wilfred, Arthur, an engineer, and one other crew member set out in the *Princess May* on the journey north to Battle Harbor. The *Albert* set out on the same day for Battle Harbor, but an ocean swell soon separated the two vessels. Wilfred skillfully guided the *Princess May* through driving wind and fog banks and around icebergs to make it safely to the sheltered water of Battle Harbor. The *Albert* had managed to make it to the harbor the day before, and Wilfred tied up alongside her. As soon as he could, Wilfred went ashore to inspect progress on the hospital.

Chapter 8

A Growing Mission

Wilfred was delighted with the progress he saw. The old house that served as the new hospital was a sturdy, two-story structure tucked close into a rocky cliff. It looked strong enough to endure even the most severe winter. Inside the building Dr. Curwen and the two nurses were working hard to set up the sixteen beds and equipment the *Albert* had brought with her. Wilfred's friend Arthur liked what he saw, too, and was eager to open the hospital doors to the fishermen and coastal people. Within a week everything was ready, and Wilfred conducted a ceremony to open the Battle Harbor Hospital.

With the new hospital open, Wilfred continued on up the Labrador coast in the *Princess May* with just one crew member, an engineer from St. John's named Paul Legget. Arthur stayed behind to help man the new hospital.

Wilfred's plan was to weave his way up through the rocky bays and inlets, going as far north as one hundred miles beyond Hopedale. He had heard of only one other steamer that had made it that far north. Along the way he would take notes on the condition of the people he met and any possible ways they could be helped to lead better lives.

One of Wilfred's first stops was Sandwich Bay, where in the 1790s an Englishman, Major Cartwright, had established a small settlement. Major Cartwright had brought four hundred people from Devon and Cornwall in England to the community to live and catch fish and trap seals. Their catches were sent back to England for sale to provide income for the community. All went well until the first years of the nineteenth century, when Britain and the United States had gone to war against each other. American privateers had captured the ships laden with goods from Sandwich Bay, and the year's earnings for the community were lost. At that time all but the most stubborn settlers returned to England, and now Wilfred visited the descendants of those who had remained to eke out a living for themselves. The people lived in a few scattered huts, having little contact with the outside world. Wilfred brought them news and medical help.

From Sandwich Bay Wilfred steamed on to Indian Harbor, where he found the *Albert* lying at anchor. Dr. Curwen and Nurse Williams were hard at work treating the injuries and ailments of the fishermen whose boats were anchored around the *Albert*. Because of the number of fishermen who had to be treated, the work of preparing the new Indian Harbor Hospital had fallen behind schedule, and Wilfred could see that the hospital would not be completed before the ice packs formed. Everyone decided it would be best to delay the official opening of the second hospital until the following year. It was decided that, instead, the *Albert* would continue sailing up and down the Labrador coast, working among the fishing fleet.

Wilfred and Paul continued their trip north. Their next stop was Rigolet, and then they steamed on to Hopedale, where they planned to rendezvous with the *Albert* once again. The voyage to Hopedale was eventful. At one point the *Princess May* found herself in a maze of reefs. Strong winds buffeted the vessel, and night began to fall. Wilfred prayed for wisdom as he shinnied up the mast in search of a way through the maze. With some deft maneuvering, he managed to reach the leeward side of an island. But Wilfred knew that the *Princess May* would not be safe there overnight. As he and Paul wondered what to do, they were relieved to see three skin-covered Eskimo boats bobbing their way toward the *Princess May*. Wilfred grinned at the Eskimos who manned the boats and threw his bowline to them. The Eskimos skillfully guided the *Princess May* into a narrow channel between the rocks where she would be safe until the buffeting winds subsided.

Wilfred transferred to one of the skin boats, which took him ashore. The Eskimos, recognizing him from his previous visit along the coast the year before, brought their sick to see him in his tent. Gangrene had set into one man's toe as a result of frostbite, and Wilfred amputated the toe on the spot. Other people had lung problems or cuts and bruises. When he had treated them all, Wilfred held a service in the tent. He knew very few words in the Inuit language, but Wilfred knew he was among the Christian converts of the Moravians, and he was glad for the unspoken fellowship.

The following morning the wind had dropped, and Wilfred was able to get back aboard the *Princess May*, where Paul had spent the night, and they continued their journey northward.

When they finally reached Hopedale, over one hundred fishing schooners were at anchor, along with the *Albert*. Eliot Curwen was already busy tending to the fishermen's medical needs, so Wilfred visited the Moravian missionaries and held services on shore. By now Wilfred Grenfell, at age twenty-eight, was something of a legend along the Labrador coast. Everyone wanted to meet him and hear him preach. Wilfred found the biggest meeting room in Hopedale and announced a meeting that night. The room was so packed that Captain Trezisse had to hold an overflow service in a nearby building.

While Wilfred was in Hopedale, he heard news of a tragedy at sea. A schooner, the *Rose*, had headed out of St. John's carrying far too many passengers and crew—sixty-two people in all. While sailing through dense fog, the vessel had hit an ice pan and crushed her bow. The *Rose* sank to the bottom eight minutes later. Men, women, and children were forced overboard into the icy water. Thankfully, another schooner soon arrived on the scene, and fifty people were rescued. But eight men, two boys, and two girls perished in the icy water.

Wilfred was furious when he heard of the tragedy, which was so avoidable. He had seen the *Rose* moored in St. John's. Not only was she an old, poorly maintained schooner but also she was far too small to carry sixty-two people. Wilfred extended his notes to include "Ways the Government can help reduce carnage at Sea." He noted that the schooners should be forbidden to carry too many passengers and that proper lifeboats and emergency equipment should be required for all those on board.

When it was time for Wilfred to leave Hopedale, one of the Moravian missionaries, a Danish man, asked if he could go along as a pilot. Wilfred readily agreed, and so the Moravian man, Paul Legget, and Wilfred all set out northward. The waters they were headed into were totally uncharted, so as a precaution Wilfred borrowed a ladder at Hopedale that he lashed to the mast so he could climb it for a better view of the treacherous reefs they would encounter.

They made it 160 miles north, all the way to Okkak, until reluctantly Wilfred turned the *Princess May* around. The water was beginning to look oily, a sure sign that it was reaching freezing point.

By the time they reached Hopedale again, most of the schooners had already headed south, and the *Albert* was pulling up anchor. Wilfred followed the *Albert*'s route, stopping in at the tiny settlements where the Liveyeres were preparing to winter.

The *Albert* and the *Princess May* met up again at Battle Harbor. Wilfred was delighted to hear that the doctors and nurses at the hospital there had been kept busy all summer. Now it was time for them to close the hospital for the winter and all head back to St. John's. Wilfred and Paul headed south in the *Princess May*, while the others traveled in the *Albert*. They had planned to rendezvous at St. Anthony Harbor, Newfoundland, before continuing to St. John's. However, they ran into foul weather, and the *Princess May* lost her mast, which was washed overboard along with the mission flag it was flying.

When he finally reached St. Anthony Harbor, Wilfred waited for several days for the *Albert* to arrive. When she did not come, he steamed out of the harbor and headed for St. John's, all the while wondering what had happened to his coworkers. When he steamed into St. John's Harbor, Wilfred saw that the *Albert* was already anchored there.

"They're alive! The doctor's alive!" The shouts went up from the pier as the *Princess May* drew closer to shore.

Wilfred soon learned that the *Princess May*'s mast and flag that had washed overboard had been found floating off the coast, and everyone assumed that the launch had been swamped in the storm and sunk. The *Albert* herself had been damaged in the storm, and Captain Trezisse had made the decision to head straight for St. John's without nearing land again.

To Wilfred's dismay, news of his "death" had already been published in the *Times* of London newspaper, and memorial services were being planned. A telegram announcing that Wilfred was alive was dispatched immediately, and Wilfred hoped that his mother was not too distraught at the erroneous story of his death.

Wilfred and his friend Arthur were soon on the move again. They had decided to visit Canada to raise money for their work in Newfoundland and Labrador. It was already growing, and Wilfred knew that the National Mission to Deep-Sea Fishermen in England could not financially sustain it much longer. He hoped to interest the Canadian government in providing five thousand dollars to build a third hospital at the inner end of Belle Isle Strait, an area within Canada's borders.

After seeing Eliot Curwen and the two nurses off to England aboard the *Albert,* Wilfred and Arthur boarded a passenger steamer for Halifax, Nova Scotia. When they arrived on December 3, 1893, they had little idea of how to proceed. They took a room in a hotel and tried to decide what to do. Eventually they settled on a simple plan. They would visit all the leading people in Halifax—government officials, the president of the board of trade, clergymen, and military officials—and ask for help. While

Wilfred fretted that this approach was too direct, without contacts or introductions it was the best they could think of to do.

The visits were more successful than Wilfred had hoped. He and Arthur were well received everywhere they went, and their message was listened to with interest. By the end of the week, a public meeting had been set up, with both the Anglican bishop and the Canadian prime minister agreeing to attend. The meeting went well, and a committee was formed to "assist the work of Dr. Grenfell."

Emboldened by the success of their time in Halifax, Wilfred and Arthur traveled on to Montreal, where they hoped to meet with Sir Donald Smith, the last resident governor of the Hudson Bay Company in Canada. As a young man, Sir Donald had been the company's manager at Hamilton Inlet, and Wilfred was sure that he was aware of the perils of living on the Labrador coast. Sir Donald had become an extremely wealthy man and was known to be interested in funding medical work.

Once again Wilfred met with success. Sir Donald agreed to meet with him and Arthur. The men talked together for several hours, swapping stories about people and places along the Labrador coast. Sir Donald introduced Wilfred and Arthur to other wealthy men, who promised to consider supporting the mission. In the meantime, Sir Donald gave Wilfred and Arthur two first-class tickets on the Canadian Pacific Railway so that they could continue their fundraising efforts all the way to Vancouver Island, on Canada's west coast.

Everywhere Wilfred and Arthur went, they were greeted by interested and enthusiastic people willing to band together to sponsor a hospital bed or a berth aboard one of the mission ships. When they got back to Montreal, good news awaited them. Sir Donald was ready to provide eighteen hundred dollars to purchase another steamer for the mission, and another man was willing to pay for a smaller sailboat. Wilfred was glad to have this news to take home with him to England.

By early March Wilfred was back in Gorleston, once again overseeing the work of the mission in the North Sea. Many things had changed in the nine months he had been away. For one thing, the copers, the small boats that supplied alcohol to the fishermen at sea, had been outlawed. In addition, more and more steam-powered trawlers were showing up on the North Sea. These new trawlers were no longer dependent on the wind to trawl and so could fish almost continuously.

As Wilfred prepared for another summer on the Labrador coast, he received some disappointing news. Arthur Bobardt announced that he was joining the navy as a surgeon, and Eliot Curwen went off to be a missionary in Peking, China. Wilfred hated to lose these two doctors, who by now knew so well the needs and conditions in Labrador, but he was relieved when two new recruits stepped forward: Dr. Fred Willway, who was on loan from the London Missionary Society, and Dr. John Bennetts, who hoped to become a permanent member of the mission.

The two new doctors, along with nurses Celia Williams and Ada Carwardine, sailed for St. John's aboard the *Albert*. However, the mission committee had decided that the *Albert* would not be staying on the Labrador coast that summer, since she was needed back in the North Sea. Instead, two new boats would be brought into service alongside the *Princess May*. The first of these new vessels was named the *Sir Donald,* after Sir Donald Smith, who had provided the money to buy her. She was a seventy-five-foot-long, fourteen-foot-wide steamer, and it was hoped that she would be fitted out and ready for service when Wilfred arrived in St. John's. The *Sir Donald* was built for the rough conditions off the Labrador coast, and she was a great improvement over the *Princess May.* The *Princess May* had been built as a river steamer, and the conditions off Labrador had pushed her beyond her limits the previous summer. By the time she had made it back to St. John's, her boiler pipes were leaking and the propeller shaft once again was bent. As a result the *Princess May* was now in dry dock undergoing a complete overhaul.

The second boat was named the *Euralia MacKinnon*. She was a sixteen-foot-long, half-decked sailboat that one of Sir Donald's associates had donated the money to buy. She had been purchased in England and would be transported to St. John's by steamer.

On June 12, 1894, Wilfred set sail for St. John's from Liverpool aboard the SS *Monica,* the *Euralia*

MacKinnon stowed safely in her hold. Traveling with him was Dr. Robert Wakefield, another of Wilfred's recruits for the summer. They arrived in St. John's twelve days later, where Wilfred was met with the now familiar rousing welcome.

The *Princess May* was still in dry dock being overhauled, and Wilfred soon learned that the *Sir Donald* was not yet ready for duty. Wilfred was anxious to get on his way up the coast, but he was forced to exercise patience. It was not until August that the *Sir Donald* was finally ready to put to sea. Eagerly Wilfred got up steam in the vessel, and they headed north. Dr. Wakefield, who was mechanically minded, served as engineer, and John Harvey, a Newfoundland captain, would serve as pilot.

Their initial destination was Battle Harbor. The *Albert* had deposited a doctor and nurse at the hospital there and at the hospital at Indian Harbor. Wilfred was anxious to see how things were progressing at both hospitals.

As they approached Battle Harbor, Wilfred decided to make a grand entrance in the new boat. "Full speed ahead," he ordered, once he thought they were clear of the rocks and reefs. They were just about to round the headland into Battle Harbor, the mission flags hoisted for the occasion flapping in the breeze, when a rumbling, grinding noise arose from the hull of the *Sir Donald*. The boat stopped abruptly and lurched to one side. It had run aground on a rock. The engine was put full astern, but the boat was stuck fast and began to be pounded by the sea. There was only one thing to do. A dinghy was lowered into the water, and Wilfred and Captain Harvey climbed aboard and rowed to shore. Once ashore they had to climb a rocky cliff to get to the community of Battle Harbor to seek help. Sheepishly Wilfred told everyone what had happened.

Baine Grieve, the merchant who had donated the building for the hospital at Battle Harbor, was visiting the community, and he raised steam in his launch and went out to pull the *Sir Donald* free of the rocks and into port.

The *Sir Donald* had been badly damaged. Her sternpost had been wrenched to one side, bashing in her rudder, and her propeller shaft had snapped and the propeller lost at sea. Wilfred was guilt-ridden as he inspected the damage that his enthusiasm to make a grand entrance had caused. It was obvious that the *Sir Donald* would be out of commission for quite some time.

Fortunately the *Albert* was still at anchor in the harbor, awaiting Wilfred's arrival. It was past time for Captain Trezisse to be heading back to England, but he agreed to tow the *Sir Donald* back to St. John's, where repairs could be made to her.

With the *Albert* needed back in England, the *Sir Donald* damaged, and the *Princess May* still months away from being fully overhauled, Wilfred had only the sailing boat the *Euralia MacKinnon* to use. Disappointed as he was at what had happened, he decided to make the most of what he had. That summer the *Euralia MacKinnon* plied the waters up and down the Labrador coast. Several Liveyeres took turns completing the two-man crew, and Wilfred enjoyed wonderful sailing conditions. It reminded him of the times he and Algernon had gone out in the *Reptile* on the estuary of the River Dee. The fact that he could take few supplies with him on the *Euralia MacKinnon* allowed Wilfred to get closer to the coastal people. After he had tended to their medical needs and held a simple church service, the local people invited him back to their homes for a meal and a good night's rest.

Wilfred visited both of the hospitals and was amazed at what the doctors and nurses had achieved. He was especially gratified to see the Indian Harbor Hospital up and running. Between them, the two hospitals had treated 1,306 patients that summer.

As winter approached, Fred Willway volunteered to stay on at Battle Harbor. He planned to take a dog team and *komatik* (sled) and visit homes along the coast when the sea froze over.

As he had done the summer before, Wilfred made notes on the people and places he visited. One particular incident that haunted his thoughts occurred when he sailed into a lonely inlet. A single hut stood by the shore, and inside Wilfred found a woman and two teenage children. Outside were three freshly dug graves. It did not take Wilfred long to learn that the husband, who had not been able to catch many fish during the summer months, had sent his wife and two oldest children down to the creek to trap fish. While they were away, he had killed himself and the two youngest children.

Wilfred gave what supplies he had to the grieving woman and her two surviving children and promised to call on them in the spring to see if they wanted to remain at the inlet or relocate to St. John's. Either way he knew their lives would be difficult. They had no one to help them, even if they went to St. John's, and the mother could not read or write. All Wilfred could do was gather the family together and pray that God would protect them until they met again.

Wilfred traveled down the Labrador coast barely ahead of the ice. As usual he was the last boat headed south. He stopped at Square Island Harbor, where twelve families lived and where things were in a desperate state. The traders who normally stopped in to exchange flour, butter, and molasses for salted fish and sealskins had all sailed right past the bay without stopping. With eight long months of winter ahead, the families were already running out of supplies.

On a previous visit to this community, Wilfred had met with a saintly old fisherman whom everyone called Uncle Jim. Now, as Uncle Jim described the situation to Wilfred, the two men knelt and prayed. Uncle Jim asked God to "open the windows of heaven and send them supplies." Wilfred agreed with a hearty amen, and the two of them waited to see what would happen next.

Wilfred spent the night at Uncle Jim's cabin, and the following morning he looked out the window to see a trading schooner at anchor! It was one of the vessels that had passed by several days before. The captain of the vessel explained that they had gotten caught in a storm and had been driven back all the way to Square Island Harbor. And now that he was there, he was happy to exchange the settlement's stockpile of dried fish and skins for flour, salt pork, and tea.

Uncle Jim grinned as he knelt to thank God for saving them all from starvation. His simple faith brought tears to Wilfred's eyes.

By October Wilfred was back in St. John's, where he learned some shocking news. The banks of Newfoundland had failed! No one could say exactly why it had happened, but businesses were bankrupt, government officials had all quit, and there were riots in the streets. The governor had urgently sent a representative to London to plead for help for the colony. Wilfred hated to leave while everything was in such an upheaval, but he had promised to be back in England by Christmas. He could only pray that things would sort themselves out. In the meantime there was little hope of getting any more financial aid from the government and the people in St. John's.

Chapter 9

Pomiuk

Wilfred arrived back in St. John's in May 1895 after a successful winter in England. Although England had not offered to bail Newfoundland out of its financial troubles, many positive steps had been taken to put the colony on a better financial footing. Canadian banks had set up shop in the colony, and the colonial secretary had pledged his private fortune to save the Commercial Bank. All of this brought a new air of confidence about the place.

The *Sir Donald* and the *Princess May* had both been repaired and were ready for a summer of service. In addition, both hospitals were equipped, and large stores of drugs, instruments, clothing, and furniture were ready for use. Wilfred was sure it was going to be the mission's best summer yet, and he was eager to take the *Sir Donald* and begin his own journey north.

At every stop along the way he found Liveyeres who were near starvation after a difficult winter. They cheered as the *Sir Donald*, her flags flying, steamed into their bays and harbors. Soon the caplin fish (smelts) arrived in hordes and piled themselves up on the beaches in their eagerness to spawn. This signaled the end of hunger for many families along the coast, and as the summer progressed, the fishing was the best in years.

It was September when Wilfred peered across the bow of the *Sir Donald* as she plowed through rough water toward the most northern point of his voyage, Nachvak Inlet. An Eskimo village was located here, along with an outpost of the Hudson Bay Company. Wilfred had heard that a man named George Ford ran the outpost, buying fox, mink, and caribou furs from the Eskimos.

It was midday before Wilfred spotted the narrow gap in the mountainous, rocky coastline that was the entrance to the inlet. Happily he turned the wheel and headed into the entrance. Once he had maneuvered inside the gap, a mile-wide fjord opened out. The water in the fjord was calm and clear, and Wilfred marveled at the four-thousand-foot-high cliffs on either side that dwarfed his boat. About halfway up the fjord he could see a long jetty and headed toward it.

By the time the *Sir Donald* pulled alongside the jetty, a group of about seventy Eskimos had gathered to meet Wilfred. Although he had not been this far north before, everyone seemed to know who he was and why he had come.

Within minutes of Wilfred's tying up the *Sir Donald*, the sick and injured were lined up for Wilfred to treat. George Ford was there, too, working alongside Wilfred, explaining the various symptoms to him and translating Wilfred's diagnoses and treatment back to the patients in their language. An hour or so later, when everyone had been seen to, Wilfred asked George if he could hold a church service. George agreed and offered his trading post as a place to do so. Once again he acted as interpreter.

The Eskimos, many of whom had been converted to Christianity through contact with the Moravian missionaries, were glad to hear a sermon. They were especially thrilled when Wilfred brought out his "magic lantern" and showed them slides depicting scenes from Bible times. They laughed at the camels and asked if they were real. The service ended with several rounds of rousing hymns, which everyone joined in singing with great enthusiasm.

By then it was dinnertime, and George invited Wilfred and the crew to eat with him and spend the night at the outpost. After they had dined on caribou steaks and dandelion leaves, which Wilfred had brought with him, Wilfred and George settled beside the iron stove for a long chat. Wilfred wanted to know about any other Eskimos George knew of who had medical needs, and George wanted the latest news from "down south."

Around midnight the conversation died down, and suddenly George's face lit up. "Ah, I almost forgot. I have a strange tale to tell you, Doctor."

Wilfred sat up a little straighter. "I like strange tales," he replied, "and there certainly are plenty to be told along this coast. Talk on."

George stood up and went to a desk, pulled out two envelopes, and sat down again. "As you can see, I have two letters here. The first one is from the Hudson Bay Company." He leaned over and showed the logo on the top of the letter to Wilfred. "The letter came by mail boat a month ago, and it asks me to do what I can to find an Eskimo boy named Pomiuk. If I find him, I am to read this second letter to him."

"Why?" Wilfred asked. "Who is Pomiuk?"

"A boy with a strange past," George replied. "His father was killed when he was very young, and his mother was taken in by another man, named Kupah. It seems that Kupah never had much time for the lad, who was left more or less to do as he pleased. Five years ago, when Pomiuk was eight years old, a white man representing the World's Fair in Chicago came to Nachvak Inlet. He brought an interpreter with him and told the locals about the great wealth that they could gain if they went back to America with him. Most of the Eskimos were too cautious to go that far from home and place their welfare in the hands of a stranger, but Kupah was greedy, and he signed both himself and Pomiuk up for the journey. The two of them ended up being part of a live exhibit of 'Eskimo Land' at the World's Fair."

Wilfred whistled. "Can you image how different that must have been for them. The food, the buildings, the climate, the huge throngs of people."

"Yes, and a lot of them wanted to prod and poke the Eskimos or watch them do tricks. Eight-year-old Pomiuk was a favorite of the crowd, especially since he could handle a dog whip so well. The people would throw coins onto a bench, and Pomiuk would pick them up with a lash of the whip." George leaned forward, opened the door of the potbelly stove, and poked the fire. "Anyway, all seemed to be going well until Pomiuk fell off a ladder and broke his thigh. Then he was useless to the exhibit, and all he could do was sit outside the Eskimo Land exhibit and beg. That is how he met the Reverend Charles Carpenter. In his younger days, Reverend Carpenter had been a missionary on the south coast of Labrador. Although he did not speak Pomiuk's language, the two became good friends. The minister would come every day to bring Pomiuk food and keep him company. However, Reverend Carpenter was only visiting the World's Fair in Chicago, and eventually he had to return home to Boston. When he left, he gave Pomiuk a photo of himself and a letter to remember him by. When the fair ended, the Eskimos were no longer needed, and they were escorted as far as St. John's and told to make their own way home from there."

Wilfred shook his head. "That's over a thousand miles!" he exclaimed.

George nodded. "I know, and Pomiuk's thigh was not properly healed. In fact, as I understand it, no one even took him to a doctor to have it looked at when the accident happened."

"So where is the boy now? He must be about thirteen," Wilfred said.

"That's the question that the Reverend Carpenter wants answered. Apparently he got one letter that Pomiuk had dictated to a passing hunter, but nothing more. So he wrote to the Hudson Bay Company, asking if they had heard anything of him. I would have said no until a week ago, when a fur trapper came in and told me that a lad who had been south was lying sick—actually dying, he said—in a tent about ten miles farther up the fjord. It sounds like it could be Pomiuk, and I'd find some way to get the letter to him if I could be sure it were him."

"How strange it must have been for the Eskimos to go to Chicago and be stared at like animals in a zoo. And then for one of them not to be taken care of properly when he got sick. That's inexcusable!" Wilfred said.

Later that night, even though Wilfred lay in a comfortable bed for the first time in weeks, he could not sleep. He could not get Pomiuk out of his mind. He prayed off and on through the night that God would guide him to the boy so that he could help him. In the morning he put a challenge to George.

"You say you think the boy is ten miles farther up the fjord. Why don't we take the *Sir Donald* up there and see if we can find him. I may be able to do something for him, and you can report back that you delivered the letter."

"It's not something I would do alone," George replied, "but I have heard so many stories of your escapades that I think I'll be safe with you. All right, let's do it together."

By lunchtime the *Sir Donald* was steaming up the fjord. Wilfred and George stood on deck taking turns using the eyeglass to scan the boulders strewn at the bottom of the rocky cliffs. Some of these boulders were twenty feet high, and Wilfred began to feel like he was looking for a needle in a haystack. The skin tent they were looking for would be well camouflaged against the grayness of the shore, and if it had been pitched on the leeward side of a boulder, they would never see it. Still, as he prayed, Wilfred felt that they should keep looking. He wasn't sure why it was so important to find one dying Eskimo boy, but deep down he knew it was.

The water was calm, and so when night fell, Wilfred anchored the *Sir Donald* close to shore and waited for first light to continue the search.

The next day George and Wilfred took a canoe ashore and climbed one of the cliffs to get a better look at what lay around them. From the cliff top Wilfred scanned the scene, taking in a huge waterfall that was cascading down a far-off cliff. As he looked, his eye rested on a tiny, pointed object near the waterfall. He adjusted the focus on his spyglass. Sure enough, it was a tent.

Jubilantly the two men clambered over to it and, after yelling a greeting, lifted the tent flap. They smelled Pomiuk before they saw him. He was covered with an old reindeer skin, and his own skin was yellow and his face drawn in pain. His hazel eyes were fixed in fear on the two visitors who had appeared from nowhere.

A woman who was in the tent with the boy sat motionless, also staring at the men. George exchanged a few words with them and nodded at Wilfred. "Yes, he is the boy we are looking for. He hasn't moved for a week, and he won't eat."

Slowly Wilfred crawled over to the boy and pulled back the reindeer skin. Pomiuk wore a fur jacket, but his bottom half was bare. Gaping wounds covered his thigh, where Wilfred supposed infection from his unhealed broken bones had set in. Without immediate help, Wilfred guessed that the boy had only hours to live.

Just then another person appeared in the tent. He introduced himself as Kupah, the boy's stepfather.

"Tell them we must take him away on the *Sir Donald* to the hospital at Indian Harbor and that we will bring him back when he is better," Wilfred instructed George.

George passed the message on to Kupah, who shrugged his shoulders. "Take him," he said. "He cannot travel on with us, and we need to get to the hunting grounds."

Very gently Wilfred lifted the reindeer skin with Pomiuk in it and backed out of the tent. He guessed the boy weighed about ninety pounds, hardly a burden to someone as physically active as Wilfred.

The two men and the boy made their way back to the canoe and then onto the *Sir Donald*. Wilfred wasted no time in washing Pomiuk and dressing his wounds. That was all he could do for now; he knew he had to get Pomiuk back to the hospital quickly.

Wilfred found a deerskin pouch hung around Pomiuk's neck. He took the pouch from him and opened it. Inside were a photograph of an elderly man and a piece of paper that turned out to be a letter from the Reverend Carpenter wishing Pomiuk well and saying that he was praying for him. Wilfred pointed to the photo and said, "Reverend Carpenter?"

Pomiuk nodded. "Yes," he said in halting English. "Me know him. Me even love him."

"And I am sure he loves you, too," Wilfred replied, surprised at how much English Pomiuk spoke.

After dropping off George, the *Sir Donald* began the voyage back to Indian Harbor. When he was not at the helm, Wilfred spent many hours tending to Pomiuk's wounds and teaching him English. Wilfred acted out many Bible stories, which made Pomiuk laugh with delight. Pomiuk also learned several hymns, and although he was still in great pain from his wounds, he often lay on his bed singing happily.

Wilfred found a lot to admire in the spunky boy he was looking after, and he prayed that Pomiuk would find Christ through the Bible stories he heard each day. When the *Sir Donald* pulled in at Hopedale to take on more coal to fire the boiler, Wilfred asked the Moravians to tell Pomiuk the gospel message in his own language. Much to everyone's delight, Pomiuk immediately accepted it and asked to be baptized. A short baptismal service was held, and Pomiuk was given the Christian name Gabriel and a concertina to accompany his energetic hymn singing.

Onward the *Sir Donald* steamed until she reached Indian Harbor, where Pomiuk was hospitalized and his leg immobilized. Wilfred wrote to the Reverend Carpenter in Boston telling him that Pomiuk, while not completely out of danger, was responding well to treatment and that he would stay at the Indian Harbor hospital through the winter.

Within two weeks a reply arrived. In the letter the Reverend Carpenter thanked Wilfred for caring for Pomiuk and asked how much it would cost to keep him in the hospital for the winter. The Reverend Carpenter went on to explain that he was the writer of the children's page in his denomination's newspaper, *The Congregationalist*. From the time he first met Pomiuk, he had written about him to the children, and now that Pomiuk had been found, hundreds of children from all over the United States were sending money and clothing for him.

What's more, the Reverend Carpenter told Wilfred that he would like to meet him, and he invited him to Boston during the winter months. Since Wilfred was already booked to speak in several Canadian cities during the winter, he decided to extend his tour to take in Boston as well. Wilfred had taken the *Sir Donald* only two hundred miles south to Battle Harbor, however, when Celia Williams sent word that Pomiuk had taken a turn for the worse and she did not know what to do with him.

Despite the coming of winter and the treacherous ice that accompanied it, Wilfred turned the steamer around and headed back to treat Pomiuk. Icicles hung from the ship's railing as they steamed northward, but they arrived in Indian Harbor without incident, and Wilfred was again able to stabilize Pomiuk. It was decided that Pomiuk would be better cared for by Dr. Robinson, who was going to spend the winter fifty miles south of Indian Harbor as a guest of the Hudson Bay Company manager at the outpost at Rigolet Harbor. The manager had a large house that he was happy to have used as a hospital through the winter.

Since the temporary hospital at Rigolet was open, Dr. Willway and Nurse Williams decided not to stay at Indian Harbor but to return to England for the winter. Dr. Willway was technically only on loan from the London Missionary Society, and he needed to report back to his mission superiors.

Wilfred took Fred Willway, Celia Williams, and Pomiuk on board and headed south as fast as the *Sir Donald's* engines would go. Along the way Pomiuk, who had learned to write and draw while hospitalized, produced a stack of drawings and letters for the Reverend Carpenter. Wilfred tucked them away in his desk, hoping to deliver them personally sometime after Christmas.

They dropped Pomiuk off at Rigolet and then steamed on to Battle Harbor, where they stopped for a quick visit with Nurse Ada Carwardine. By now snow was falling and ice fingers were reaching out from land into the sea. The fishing schooners had all gone south for the winter, and only the Liveyeres and a few Eskimos remained to winter along the coast.

Nurse Carwardine had agreed to stay in Battle Harbor for the winter and keep the hospital open. Wilfred admired her courage; it was going to be a long, lonely winter for her. She would be the first nurse ever to winter over on the Labrador coast. She was already finding it a challenge to keep herself and the hospital warm. The missionaries held a service and prayed for her before they hurried back on board the *Sir Donald,* hoping to beat the ice packs that were growing by the minute.

Wilfred set course for St. Anthony, on the northern tip of Newfoundland island. He dropped off Celia and Fred so they could take the faster mail steamer to St. John's. From there they would take an Allen Line ship to London. Wilfred sent a letter with them to the mission council, explaining that he was going to spend the winter in Canada and the United States raising awareness and, he hoped, funds for the mission.

After the mail steamer left, Wilfred made his way along the Newfoundland coast, finally arriving at St. John's. He held several meetings and did follow-up treatment on many of the fishermen who had been treated by the mission's doctors over the summer. When he had done all he could, he took a passenger ship to Halifax, Canada, to begin his winter speaking tour.

Of all the stories Wilfred told when he spoke, he soon discovered that Pomiuk's was the one that touched people's hearts. He traveled to Montreal and then to Toronto. He thanked God for the great success that his time in Canada had been. He had no idea that it would soon be overshadowed by his visit to Boston.

In early January 1896, Wilfred crossed the border and entered the United States of America for the first time. He then took a train to Boston.

It seemed to Wilfred that the Reverend Carpenter knew everyone in the city, and the hearts of thousands of people had already been stirred by the story of Pomiuk. When Wilfred spoke at the minister's church, all of the pews filled up quickly and people stood at the back for the entire service. Each speaking engagement the Reverend Carpenter arranged for Wilfred led to three more, and soon Wilfred was the talk of the town. Newspapers carried headlines telling where Wilfred was speaking and what he was expected to say.

One young woman, Emma White, attended many of Wilfred's meetings. She was the librarian at the Congregational Church headquarters in Boston, and she was so enthusiastic about helping the people of Newfoundland and Labrador that she offered to set up a committee to support Wilfred's work there. Another friend of the Reverend Carpenter, Arthur Estabrook, who was a leading banker in the city, offered to serve on the committee and to finance an office for it.

When it came time to leave Boston, Wilfred was humbled by all of the interest in his work. Hundreds of church leaders had asked him what they could do to help, and he told them all the same thing: Come and help if you can; pray and give if you can't. Wilfred knew that most of the interest that had been stirred up was a direct result of his going to find Pomiuk. He thanked God that he had felt compelled to search for the boy.

Wilfred's success in Boston led to an invitation to speak in New York City. Wilfred decided to make the most of the opportunity and headed south. When he arrived in New York, two letters were waiting for him. The first was from the council of the National Mission to Deep-Sea Fishermen. As Wilfred ripped it open, a chill went down his spine. He read, "Dr. Grenfell, you are requested to return home, if at all possible in time for the Annual Meeting, in order that the Council might make arrangements for you to conduct ALL of your future work in England."

The second letter was from his old friend and mentor Dr. Treves, who tried to explain to Wilfred why he was being recalled to England. "You have established the mission in Labrador," Wilfred read, "and done the pioneer work, but the North Sea is suffering. Things are not going so well at Gorleston, and as a matter of duty you ought to return." The word *duty* was underlined.

Wilfred knew he had to return to England, but he had one more thing he felt he had to do first. He wanted to sail aboard a sealing ship to document the conditions the men worked under and to test the possibilities of sending missionaries out on the sealing ships themselves. He was aware it would be a particularly dangerous assignment, but he felt that someone had to do it, and Wilfred never asked another missionary to do something he was not willing to do himself.

Chapter 10

Seal Hunt

At noon on March 30, 1896, the church bells of St. John's pealed loudly. Wilfred stood on the deck of the *Greenland*, crammed in alongside three hundred seal hunters. A huge cheer went up from them all as the bells rang out—the signal that the five-week seal-hunting season had officially begun. Ship sirens wailed and flags fluttered in the stiff breeze.

Finally, after years of hearing about it, Wilfred was on his way to a seal hunt. When he first arrived in St. John's four years before, he learned that in mid-February huge ice pans broke off from the Arctic ice sheet and were driven south by the spring winds. Perched on these ice pans were hundreds of thousands of hood and harp seals that hitched a ride all the way to Belle Isle Strait, between Newfoundland

and Labrador, where the winds died down and the ice pans bobbed about in one place. There the female seals gave birth to their whelps. The baby seals thrived on the ice pans, and within a month they weighed as much as fifty pounds. It was then, when the whelps were large enough to catch fish for themselves, that the seal-hunting season was declared open.

Steam was quickly raised, and soon twenty or more ships were jostling for position to clear the bottleneck exit of St. John's Harbor. The *Greenland* took her place between the *Neptune* and the *Windsor* as she lined up to pass between the cliffs and race toward Belle Isle Strait for her share of the seal pelts.

With the exception of his doctor's satchel, which he had slung over his shoulder, Wilfred looked just like his fellow seal hunters, dressed in thick woolen pants and jacket, fur cap, and knee-high boots. As the *Greenland* headed for open water, Wilfred moved among the seal hunters, reacquainting himself with those he had met before when they worked on fishing boats over the summer and introducing himself to unfamiliar faces. The atmosphere was electric; adrenaline ran high. If things went well, the sealers would have money to buy fishing equipment for the summer's fishing. If things did not go well, they and their families would struggle until next year, when they would head out again for another chance at the seal pelts.

The *Greenland* made swift progress. The first night out from St. John's, everyone who was not on watch slept on a straw mattress in the hold. It was a luxury to be inside. As soon as the holds started to fill with seal pelts, the crew would have to sling their mattresses down on the frozen deck and sleep there.

The next morning Wilfred was up bright and early. He did his usual exercise routine and followed it up with a dousing of icy water. As the others awoke, he lashed a ladder he had brought with him to the center mast. Then he climbed to the top rung, and with one arm hooked inside the rung for support against the rolling of the ship, he preached his first sermon of the voyage. It was short and to the point, something that each man, no matter how educated, could identify with. Then he climbed down, handed out some hymnals, and started singing. Many of the men joined in, and soon the ship was vibrating with hymns.

Once the service was over, Wilfred joined the other men scrubbing the deck and untangling ropes. As he did so, he kept an eye out for the sealers who wanted to discuss his message further. He found several men who were ready to listen as he told them about his Christian faith.

The *Greenland* and several other ships reached the strait at the same time. Wilfred peered over the side at an amazing sight. Carried by the wind and the tide, huge ice pans swished back and forth in the water. The captain climbed the rigging and scrambled into a large basket lashed to the masthead. He pulled an eyeglass out of his pocket and began combing the scene.

"Twenty degrees north," he yelled. "It's a wide vein. Should take us a way."

Wilfred watched as the helmsman turned the wheel and the *Greenland* began to move to a northerly heading as she crashed through a thin ice pan. He said a quick prayer under his breath. He knew that this was the most dangerous part of the voyage. The captain was looking for veins or paths through the ice, but if the wind changed, those veins could close up in an instant, crushing a ship like a walnut. Wilfred listened as the hull creaked and groaned, but it held, and the ship steamed on into the northerly vein.

Then the captain yelled, "Seals ahead, lads. Prepare to go over."

In an instant hundreds of men sprang into action. They grabbed their equipment—a club or pole to kill the seals and a length of rope with which to drag the skins back to the ship—and a small canvas bag containing their food ration, a mixture of oatmeal and sugar that they could moisten with melted ice and eat out on the ice pan.

Wilfred planned to go over the side with the sealers, not with a hunting kit but with his medical bag. He knew that there would be many injuries as the men worked to catch as many seals as they could.

As he looked out across the ice pans, Wilfred saw thousands of big, brown seals, many with white-coated whelps at their sides. It was an awesome sight, and for a brief moment he wished his father were at his side. Wilfred's father had loved geography and would have been fascinated to see something that he had only read about.

But there was little time to reflect on the past; while 280 of the men were climbing down ropes onto the ice, the remaining twenty men would take their turn staying with the ship. Wilfred grabbed his bag and his food ration and joined the throng. When he stood on the ice pan, he found it was not as smooth as it looked from the ship. In fact it was quite broken up, with large, jagged points. Running and falling on it was a sure formula for gashed legs.

The men roped themselves together in pairs. That way, if one sealer went through the ice, he had a chance of being pulled out. If they both fell together, there was little hope for either man. Wilfred did not have a partner, so he stayed close behind the men, following in their exact footsteps.

Soon the hunt began. The men went after the seals with white fur first and removed their pelts on the spot. The pelts were piled up and pulled back to the *Greenland,* where they were stowed in the hold.

Wilfred watched the scene with fascination until the wounded started to call for him. Some sealers had cut themselves on the ice, others with the knives they used to skin the seals. Still others had dislocated or broken ankles from running across the uneven surface. All the men were grateful to have the doctor right there with them. They hoped he could patch them up well enough so they could go on with the hunt. And no wonder, Wilfred told himself. The white pelts fetched up to ten shillings each at market. There was nothing else these men could do that would bring in that kind of money so fast.

Wilfred was busy until late afternoon, when the wind suddenly died. He looked up to see that the *Greenland* had disappeared over the horizon. He and about thirty men around him were alone on the ice together. It was a sobering moment, but Wilfred knew they must not panic. The captain knew where they were, and he would come back for them as soon as he could find a vein to work the ship through. In the meantime cold was their greatest enemy. The men had dressed thinly to run across the ice, and now as night descended they were beginning to shiver. Every year men were left behind and froze to death on the ice, and Wilfred had no intention of being one of them.

Thankfully, the men were on a large ice pan, large enough for them to exercise on. Wilfred started a game of leapfrog to keep them all warm. Darkness finally fell. The men smeared seal fat on their wooden poles and then set fire to them to attract the attention of the ship. The hours slipped by, and Wilfred kept the men exercising, singing, and praying until, around midnight, they saw the distant lights of the *Greenland*. The ship inched toward them, and by one o'clock the men were safely back on board. By now several of them were frostbitten, and Wilfred got them below deck for treatment.

As the days carried on in an efficient pattern of hunting, skinning, and stowing seal pelts, Wilfred's medical skills were needed often.

Sunday was the day the law decreed that no seal hunting be carried out. Wilfred conducted an extra long service in the morning and looked forward to spending time talking to the men on deck in the afternoon. But it was not to be. Soon after lunch the watch spotted a group of about twenty men toiling across the ice. Wilfred and the sealers watched as they grew closer and finally came within shouting range.

"Where are you from?" the captain yelled.

"Off the SS *Wolf,*" was the reply. "She's gone down, and we've fanned out to get help."

Soon the men were drinking hot tea on board the *Greenland* and telling their story. Early in the morning a breeze from the south had driven the ice away from the southern shore of Fogo Island. The *Wolf* was working her way successfully north between the island and the ice flow when the wind changed, driving the ice back toward the shore. The *Wolf* was trapped. The captain tried to maneuver his ship into a small, iced-over indentation in the cliff face. It was not enough to keep the ship safe, but it did give the men time to scramble overboard before the impact of the ice crushed the ship, sending her to the bottom of the ocean.

The men reported that just about everyone had made it over the side, but the others were all adrift on the ice and needed to be picked up as soon as possible. All hands were called for, and the *Greenland* steamed off in the direction of the island.

As Wilfred manned the ropes, he thought of all the hopes that had been crushed along with the SS

Wolf. Three hundred sealers were now penniless, and their captain ruined, all because of the power of the ice.

Later that day the *Greenland* and several other sealing ships picked up the men from the SS *Wolf*.

The hunting went on, and by the time the *Greenland* headed back to St. John's, pelts worth forty-three thousand dollars were safely stowed in her hold. Although Wilfred had put his other duties first, he had still managed to bring back his share of pelts to the ship, a fact that impressed the men. When they reached port, the men took up a collection and handed Wilfred thirty-seven dollars for the mission fund. They told him they were grateful to have a doctor and a minister on board and encouraged him to come back the following year. Wilfred said he would try, but the letter from the mission committee weighed heavily on his heart.

As the ocean liner that was taking him back to England slipped out of St. John's Harbor, Wilfred wondered whether he would ever again see the people and the coast that had become so dear to him.

Chapter 11

Red Bay Cooperative Society

On May 1, 1896, Wilfred stood before the council of the National Mission to Deep-Sea Fishermen giving a report on the work in Newfoundland and Labrador. For the most part, the council was impressed with all that had been done and the money Wilfred had raised in Canada and the United States. But the council did have one problem with Wilfred's work. While he was away, the mission council had come to the conclusion that the work across the Atlantic Ocean had become too closely linked with the name Wilfred Grenfell. To illustrate their concern, the council produced letters that had been addressed to "The Grenfell Mission," when in fact they were meant for the National Mission to Deep-Sea Fishermen.

It seemed to Wilfred that this matter had been well discussed before he arrived back in England and that the council had already reached a conclusion. Sure enough, Wilfred was told that the council had decided to appoint Dr. Fred Willway to take over the mission's work in Labrador and Newfoundland. Wilfred would be allowed to return to Labrador for one last summer to instruct his successor.

Wilfred was disappointed by this turn of events, but he tried to look on the bright side. He admired Fred a great deal and knew that he would make a fine leader for the work. And Wilfred had one last summer to set some of his boldest ideas in motion!

After a quick visit with his mother and brother in Parkgate, Wilfred set out once again across the Atlantic. Fred accompanied him; his wife would join him in Newfoundland later. On the voyage the two men spent many hours on deck discussing the future of the mission's work in Labrador.

Wilfred longed for a time when there would be no starvation on the coast, when men could find work during the winter months as well as the summer, and when children could go to school. In his mind this all depended on one thing—breaking the power of the schooner owners and fish traders along the coast. In the four years that Wilfred had been working in Labrador, he had learned that certain traders controlled portions of the coastline and that all of the fishermen in that area had to sell their catch to them. The traders set the price, and if the fishermen went looking for a better price somewhere else, they were blacklisted and never allowed to sell their fish to that trader or any of his friends again. Wilfred had seen cases where a desperate fisherman had bartered some of his catch for milk for his children and in retaliation the trader had refused to sell him powder for his gun. This meant that the fisherman could not hunt for food during the winter months.

This all led to a situation wherein the fishermen were virtually owned by the traders who loaned them money to buy equipment at the start of the fishing season and at the end of the season sold them food and supplies at exorbitant prices to tide them over for the winter.

One fisherman acting alone could not break this system; it would crush him. The answer, Wilfred told Fred, was for the fishermen to band together into cooperatives. In fact, Wilfred had already suggested such an idea to the fishermen at Red Bay. He was eager to meet with them again and see how far they were prepared to go in setting up their own trading store in the bay and working directly with merchants in St. John's.

As soon as they reached Newfoundland, Wilfred and Fred took the *Sir Donald* north. The ice had receded early, and they had no difficulty reaching Red Bay in good time. At Red Bay, on the north side of the Strait of Belle Isle, Wilfred gathered the men of the community together in an old fish shed.

"Have you thought about what I told you?" Wilfred asked the fishermen.

At first no one said anything; they all just moved uncomfortably in their seats and looked at one another. No one seemed to want to be the first to speak. Wilfred understood why. If it got back to the traders that the fishermen had spoken out against the way they did business, they might retaliate against the fishermen. Finally one old fisherman spoke up.

"I've been thinking long about it, Doctor, and I think you be right. It is time for some different way to be doing things. Here be my investment in the co-op. It not be much, and if I had more, I would gladly give ye it." The man handed eight dollars to Wilfred.

Spurred on by the old fisherman's example, other men began to stand and affirm the idea, handing over what money they had been able to save toward the project during the previous year.

When everyone had contributed his share toward the cost of establishing the co-op, it totaled eighty-five dollars. It was not nearly enough to cover all the costs, but Wilfred pledged money of his own for the project, and he had already received a pledge from three merchants in St. John's that they too would support the project.

"I know this step has not been easy for you to take," Wilfred said. "I respect your courage in deciding to move ahead. With God's help we will see a wonderful new and honest way of buying and selling develop. Now, let me explain some of the rules of the cooperative to you."

Wilfred laid out the rules of the new Red Bay Cooperative Society. The members of the society would be the heads of the families of the community, and they would appoint the storekeeper. All goods would be sold for cash; there would be no credit. The goods sold in the co-op store would be sold at cost plus the price of freight from St. John's plus five percent for the storekeeper and five percent to build up a cash reserve in the society. This would still make goods much cheaper than the price the traders normally charged for them. In addition, the members of the society agreed to sell their fishing catches to the cooperative. The fish would be shipped to St. John's and sold for a fair price on the market, not the paltry sum the traders gave them for their catch.

The men were happy with these rules, and they elected William Pike, a well-respected fisherman in the community, to be the storekeeper of the new cooperative.

When the meeting was over, Wilfred went outside and in chalk wrote on the side of the building in large block letters, RED BAY COOPERATIVE STORE. The men smiled and clapped each other on the back when they saw it.

It took a good part of the summer for Wilfred to get the cooperative up and running properly. Once it was operating, Wilfred sailed north to visit the Moravian missionaries one last time. When he arrived, Wilfred found his presence was sorely needed. An epidemic of scarlet fever was raging through the community, and he set to work caring for those with the disease.

As summer drew to a close, it was time to turn the *Sir Donald* around and head for St. John's again.

When Wilfred arrived there, good news awaited. The mission was now officially known as the Royal National Mission to Deep-Sea Fishermen. The word *royal* added to the name meant that the mission now carried Queen Victoria's personal endorsement.

A letter was also awaiting Wilfred, saying that the mission considered this a good time for Wilfred to make another fundraising drive into Canada and the United States before returning to England.

Wilfred was glad for the opportunity to visit many old friends, and he set off enthusiastically on a fall tour. His journey took him from Halifax to Montreal, and then on to Boston, where the Reverend Carpenter and Emma White had once again arranged a busy schedule of meetings for him. Another Christian man was holding meetings in Boston at the time—none other than Dwight L. Moody. It had been fourteen years since Wilfred had heard Moody speak in East London, but he had never forgotten what Moody had said. Now Wilfred determined to go and thank the man for the way his message had changed not only his life but also the lives of countless others through him.

It was a blustery Thursday night when Wilfred made his way to Tremont Temple, where D. L. Moody was to preach. Wilfred explained who he was to one of the ushers at the door. He was quickly whisked backstage to talk to the famous evangelist before the service began.

Dwight Moody looked a little older and broader, but other than that, he was much as

Wilfred remembered him. After a brief introduction, Wilfred got straight to the point. "I want to tell you that fourteen years ago I received inspiration from you to serve Jesus Christ," he said.

"Wonderful," Moody replied. "And what have you been doing since?"

"Well," Wilfred said, "I have been preaching the gospel on the Labrador coast. I became a doctor so that I could tend men's bodies and a preacher so that I could touch their souls."

"Very good," Moody said as he straightened his tie.

An assistant popped his head around the curtain and said, "It's time to start, sir."

"Just give me a minute," he replied. Then D. L. Moody turned to Wilfred and asked, "And do you regret that you are not a successful Harley Street doctor, eating delicate dinners and wearing a silk beaver hat?"

"Not at all," Wilfred said. "I have no regrets."

"Well, then, Doctor," Moody said as he slapped Wilfred on the shoulder, "come out there with me and tell the people what a joy it is to serve Jesus Christ."

The next thing Wilfred knew he was on stage, singing his favorite hymns along with an audience of hundreds. When the singing was over, Dwight Moody introduced him to the crowd, and Wilfred got his opportunity to speak.

Wilfred started by briefly describing his mission work along the Labrador coast. Then he went on to say, "I am grateful for Mr. Moody's life. Everything that I have done that is worthwhile in this world I owe to his preaching. When you and I come to the end of life, supposing that we had had all the wealth in the world, would we look back and say that that brought us satisfaction? Can you measure success in that way? If there is a poor child in Labrador dying because he has no food or a young fellow here in Boston going down to hell because he has no one to show him the way to heaven, wouldn't serving those people be a better way to live than hoarding wealth?

"Looking back on the little things in life, I had rather have them than all the gold. When we come before the judgement seat at the day of reckoning, we shall measure our success in no other way than by what the gospel of Jesus Christ has enabled us to do. Christ has led me to some of the bleakest places on earth, but I have never been sorry that I obeyed His call. The truth is, I don't have to wait until heaven to get my rewards. I get them every day in the satisfaction of helping people and knowing that I am doing something the Master approves of. That is what He did while He was here on earth—He helped people, and if we want to follow Him, that is what we have to do, too."

Wilfred was glad that he'd had the opportunity to meet D. L. Moody again and thank him for being a link in the chain of people who had helped him find his life's work.

In Boston Wilfred also spoke at Harvard University, and then he traveled on to speak at

Yale. His final stop in the United States was New York City, where large crowds came out to hear him speak.

On February 14, 1897, Wilfred Grenfell watched the Statue of Liberty disappear from view over the stern of the steamer. Once again he was headed for England, ready to take up the challenges that lay ahead for him there.

Chapter 12

A Single Letter Changed Everything

Wilfred had been back in England for only six months when he picked up his pen to write an article for *Toilers of the Deep*. He began, "Obviously the most important problem the mission has to solve in the near future is how shall we adapt ourselves to the exigencies of steam trawling."

It was a problem that had gripped Wilfred from the moment he set foot back on English soil. The old sailing smacks were now a thing of the past. In just a few years, they had gone from being the mainstay of British fisheries, setting sail with great fanfare and flag waving, to rotting away at their docks in ports around the country. Steam trawlers, with their iron hulls and bright lights, were able to weather all conditions and trawl for twenty-four hours a day until their holds were filled and they returned home with their catch. Because of this, the fishermen did not have time for the mission ships to visit, nor could the mission ships, which were still mostly sailing vessels, keep up with them. It was time for a change in strategy.

Wilfred and the mission committee wrestled with the problem for a year before agreeing to move the mission's emphasis to land. They decided to build bigger and better recreation/mission halls in port cities so that fishermen would have an alternative to frequenting the hundreds of pubs that vied for their business.

While he was touring the British Isles raising money for the new mission halls, Wilfred never forgot to mention the doctors and nurses who were working faithfully across the Atlantic Ocean in Labrador. He desperately wanted to send a well-equipped hospital ship to aid their work, and he set about raising the three thousand pounds needed to buy such a vessel.

As he spoke about his time in Labrador, Wilfred realized that his heart was still with the people there, though he had resigned himself to taking his orders from the mission committee in London.

Then, in July 1899, a single letter changed everything. The letter was from Dr. Fred Willway, and in it he reported that his wife was seriously ill and needed to return to Great Britain for a long period of rest. Dr. Willway was asking to be relieved of his post as director of the work in Newfoundland and Labrador.

Wilfred's pulse raced as he read the letter, but he tried not to get his hopes up. Perhaps, he told himself, just perhaps he would be allowed to go back and lead the work there. Sure enough, Wilfred's name was proposed as a replacement for Fred Willway. And when a vote was taken, Wilfred had the job! He hardly knew what to do first, he was so excited at the thought of returning to the rugged coastline that had been the focus of so many of his dreams in recent years.

It was a perfect time for Wilfred to leave for Labrador, because the money for the new hospital ship had come in and by the end of summer the ship would be outfitted and ready for service. The vessel was named the *Strathcona*, after Sir Donald Smith, who was now Lord Strathcona. Sir Donald had paid a generous portion of the cost to purchase the ship.

Wilfred could not wait until the *Strathcona* was finished and ready to put to sea. He and Andrew Beattie, a Scottish fisherman friend, took passage on the first ship they could find, an ore-carrying steamer bound for Tilt Cove, on the eastern coast of Newfoundland. Once there, the two men would wait for one of the mission's ships, the *Julia Sheridan*, to pick them up and take them north to Labrador.

Everything went as planned, and Wilfred arrived back on the coast he loved so much in early September 1899. The residents at Tilt Cove welcomed him with open arms, and when the *Julia Sheridan* arrived to pick up the two men, they gave generous supplies of food and coal to send the vessel with their doctor aboard on its way.

Wilfred arrived in Battle Harbor on September 25. He was delighted to see the hospital full and functioning efficiently. Dr. Apsland, one of the new batch of doctors, had married Nurse Ada Carwardine, and the couple worked happily together at this remote location.

As the hospitals grew, the mission had gained a new level of respect, and soon after Wilfred arrived back, the government of Newfoundland announced that each mission doctor was automatically accorded the position of justice of the peace. Since there were no policemen on the coast, this was an important position. It empowered the doctors to settle disputes or refer to the courts in St. John's those that could not be settled or were criminal acts.

One other aspect of being a justice of the peace was particularly exciting to Wilfred. Any kind of alcohol was illegal on the Labrador coast, but ships from Nova Scotia still brought it in, and many Liveyeres had stills hidden along the rocky coastline. Since his earliest days with the mission on the North Sea, when the mission ships had to compete with the coper boats, Wilfred had hated what alcohol did to the fishermen and their families. It caused accidents and fights and left women without money for food and children without fathers. Now, at last, the mission could play an active role in keeping alcohol off the Labrador coast.

As Wilfred headed north up the Labrador coast in the *Julia Sheridan*, his excitement mounted as he came up with a plan to fulfill a long-term dream. This winter, for the first time, he planned to stay over in Newfoundland. A trader named George Moore had invited Wilfred to stay with him at St. Anthony, located at the northern tip of Newfoundland island. The community at St. Anthony had also been asking the mission to place a hospital in their bay for some time, and over the past two years, Dr. Willway had allowed a mission doctor to stay there. The doctors had proved to be an invaluable resource to the people for miles around.

Now Wilfred wanted to see firsthand what could be done for the people during the winter months. He laid up the *Julia Sheridan* in the harbor at St. Anthony for the winter and set up a surgery unit in George Moore's back room. His friend and traveling companion, Andrew Beattie, opened up a school to which thirty children flocked. The children were grateful for something to do over winter, and every recess was a wonderful treat for them. The boys of Mostyn House School had sent out ten soccer balls with Wilfred, who set about teaching everyone how to play soccer on the ice. The game became so popular that old men left their sickbeds to take up the sport and young mothers, with their babies strapped to their backs, giggled and whooped as they passed the ball to their team members.

During this time Wilfred also set out to master a new skill—dogsledding. Dogsleds were the main form of transportation in Newfoundland and on the Labrador coast during the winter. Wilfred knew that if he were to visit sick patients in outlying areas, he needed to know how to work a dog team. He soon found that it was not as easy as it looked. Eight to ten dogs were harnessed to a komatik, a long, narrow dogsled, by traces (straps) made of walrus hide. With the dogs harnessed to the sled, the driver would yell "Oo-isht," and the dogs would run off, pulling the sled behind them. The first few times Wilfred tried this, his attempts ended in a tangle of dogs and traces, the sled on its side and Wilfred facedown in a snowbank. On one occasion half the dogs went one way around a tree and the rest the other! But slowly Wilfred got the hang of it. He learned how to keep his balance and how to make the dogs do what he wanted them to do. Soon he was confidently racing across snow and ice with a dog team and komatik.

Opportunities for Wilfred to use his komatik and dogs soon presented themselves, and he was off across the bay ice to one emergency after another. During the winter he traveled over sixty miles in each direction and performed operations on rough-hewn kitchen tables and benches. Once the patient had been attended to, Wilfred would normally settle in for an overnight visit. He loved to listen to the locals tell their stories of living in the north and their half-remembered tales from their distant ancestral lands of Ireland, Scotland, and France. Wilfred ended each visit with a Bible reading and prayer, encouraging his ever-growing circle of friends to have faith in God.

Wilfred loved staying in St. Anthony just as much as he enjoyed his mercy dashes across the white countryside. Using his newly bestowed powers as a justice of the peace, he turned the little-used courthouse and jail into a community clubroom. He papered it with old magazines and brightly illustrated Bible texts. Local people donated tables and chairs, and soon, for the first time, the people of St. Anthony met together to play games and read magazines and books.

Christmas 1899 and New Year 1900 were two celebrations that would live long in the memory of everyone present. In December Wilfred insisted on cutting down a tree and decorating it, a wonder the children had never seen before. New Year's Day brought with it a huge sports gala, with obstacle races in which the competitors had to scramble over a wrecked schooner that was stuck in the ice and crawl under seal nets.

Such activities helped to pass the long winter, and more important to Wilfred, they got the locals thinking about themselves as a group. This was important to him because toward the end of winter he hoped to get enough volunteers together to go inland and cut down trees to start building a hospital in the community. It would be muscle-straining work, and Wilfred had no money to offer the people for their effort, only the satisfaction of helping their community and the communities around them.

When the time came for the tree felling, Wilfred was delighted with everyone's team spirit. In just a month, over 350 large trees were felled, trimmed, and carted by komatik back to the hospital site. The building itself would have to wait until next winter because it was now time for the people of St. Anthony to prepare for the fishing season.

Wilfred and Andrew set about preparing the *Julia Sheridan* for another summer of mission work. As soon as the ice was gone, they set off north for a tour along the Labrador coast. Wilfred was delighted to find that the Red Bay Cooperative was running well and that, with the good prices the co-op got for their fish, the members of the community had enjoyed their best winter ever. Everyone had enough food and clothing, and there was even money left over to buy new fishing supplies. For the first time in memory, the fishermen did not start the new season in debt to the traders. Wilfred encouraged the men to spread the news of their success to other fishermen they met that summer. He hoped that this would stir up interest and there would be a string of co-ops along the coast by fall.

In August Wilfred was back in Battle Harbor for the arrival of the *Strathcona*. The vessel was quite a sight tied up alongside the wharf in the bay. She was ninety-seven feet long and had a steel hull, reinforced for work in the ice. Her lines were sleek, and she was rigged as a ketch, with masts fore and aft. Her funnel was set midway along the ship. She could make five knots using her steam engine and nine knots if the sails were raised to help the steam engine power her forward.

Wilfred had worked hard to raise the money to buy the ship, and he eagerly clambered aboard to check her out. Her decks were teak, and the wood below deck was polished mahogany. Below deck and just forward of amidships and the engine room was a spacious hospital with six beds, a dispensary, and X-ray equipment. In the rear was a saloon and crew quarters. The ship was also fitted with the latest conveniences, such as electric lights and bathrooms. On deck, all the brass fittings were polished to a gleaming shine, and engraved on her large steering wheel were the words "Follow Me, and I will make you fishers of men."

Wilfred took up residence in one of the *Strathcona's* new cabins and spent the rest of the summer traveling up and down the coast, visiting the mission's hospitals, making new friends, and dreaming of ways to help the local people.

There were still many tragic incidents, all of which Wilfred recorded in his log. In one case Wilfred helped a three-year-old girl whose feet had been severely frostbitten. The frostbite had turned to gangrene, and the girl's father, rightly fearing that she would die if nothing were done, had chopped off both her feet at the ankles. When Wilfred found the girl he took her to Battle Harbor Hospital, where the wounds were cleaned up and she was fitted with a pair of hand-carved wooden feet.

It was this girl's plight and the plight of other children that touched Wilfred the most. At another remote inlet, a woman handed him two baby girls, saying, "They're twins. I know there's somethin' wrong with 'em, though I don't know what. Here, you take 'em. I've got seven others, and I can't raise these two as well."

Wilfred took the two little girls and observed their behavior. He soon concluded that the mother had been correct. There was something wrong with them: they were both blind.

There were many other children, orphaned, abandoned, or too ill for their parents to care for them. Wilfred welcomed them all aboard the *Strathcona* and cared for them as best he could. When he got back to St. John's he wrote to various friends in the United States, Canada, and England, urging them to find adoptive homes for the children. Eventually many of the children did get sent on to better lives elsewhere. However, one of Wilfred's dreams was to have an orphanage somewhere along the coast so that the children did not have to be relocated. It was just one of many schemes Wilfred had rolling around inside his head for Labrador and Newfoundland.

In 1902 Wilfred had an unexpected opportunity to do something about the illegal liquor trade on the Labrador coast. In late summer that year, an English barquentine, the *Bessie Dodd*, had been reported wrecked at Smoky Tickle, at the entrance to Hamilton Inlet. The vessel's captain and owner had made an insurance claim with Lloyds of London for the loss of the boat. But Lloyds was suspicious of the claim and sent a cable to Wilfred asking if he would investigate the wreck.

Wilfred had already laid up the *Strathcona* in St. John's Harbor for the winter, but the cable had piqued his interest. Despite the fact that it was already November 15 and the sea was beginning to ice over, he decided to investigate. He chartered a steam trawler named the *Magnific* and set out for Smoky Tickle. It was tough going. Fierce winds blew, buffeting the boat, and the crew was kept busy chipping away ice lest she become top-heavy and capsize.

Despite the weather, they made it to Smoky Tickle, where they found the *Bessie Dodd* aground.

"It looks to me like a crime has taken place," Wilfred said to the captain of the *Magnific* as the two grim-faced men stood onshore inspecting the *Bessie Dodd*.

"Aye," the captain replied. "What ship runs aground one hundred and fifty feet from the wharf where she's taken on her cargo of fish? And on a flat, sandy beach no less. And look, the only damage seems to be a broken steering chain."

Despite the broken steering chain's being the only damage, the ship's captain had sold the *Bessie Dodd* for eighty dollars to Gerry Jewett, the trader whose cargo he had taken on board. When he got back to England, the captain had made a claim to Lloyds for fifteen thousand dollars to cover the cost of his vessel and another twenty thousand dollars for the loss of the cargo he was carrying. And with the ship's being in such a remote location with winter setting in, the captain had expected Lloyds to pay his claim without investigating the loss.

Using all his skill as a mariner, the captain of the *Magnific* maneuvered his vessel around, and a towline was attached to the *Bessie Dodd*. Inch by inch the vessel was pulled off the beach and back into the water. The sailing conditions were foul, and several times Wilfred thought he might have to cut the line and let the *Bessie Dodd* float freely, but the *Magnific* and her charge made it back to St. John's.

The authorities at St. John's were surprised to see the *Bessie Dodd* afloat. An investigation was quickly mounted, and the original owner of the vessel was brought from England to stand trial for fraud. When the owner arrived in St. John's, he confessed that he and Jewett had colluded to defraud Lloyds of London.

Wilfred could not have been happier with this outcome. Jewett had illegally been supplying alcohol along the Labrador coast for years, and this was just the opportunity to be rid of him.

Jewett was immediately arrested and stood trial with the *Bessie Dodd*'s original owner. Both men were found guilty of fraud and sent to prison. With Gerry Jewett behind bars, Wilfred headed to St. Anthony, where the hospital was now completed, to spend the winter.

Chapter 13

Adrift

By 1905 the work in Labrador and Newfoundland was growing by leaps and bounds. The mission council had dropped any plans to have Wilfred return to England and carry on his work with the mission there. Wilfred Grenfell was now as much a part of the Labrador coast as any fisherman who had been born and raised there, and he never wanted to leave the place again.

With the hospital at St. Anthony now well established, Wilfred had made that community his winter headquarters. During the summer months he took the *Strathcona* and served the fishing fleet and those living in the most remote areas of Labrador and Newfoundland. The hospitals at Battle Harbor and Indian Harbor were extended, and a string of nursing stations was established along the coast. A hardy nurse manned each station through the winter, and a succession of volunteer medical students and nurses staffed them in the summer. These volunteers were Wilfred's pride and joy. He called them WOPS, which stood for "workers without pay."

Every time Wilfred went on a speaking engagement to Canada or the United States, hundreds of people asked him how they could help. He always invited them to come to the mission and use whatever skills they had, and by 1905 hundreds had taken up the challenge. At times the number of volunteers overwhelmed the full-time workers and tensions rose between the two groups, but it never bothered Wilfred. He was glad to introduce young people to the rigors of missionary service, and their enthusiasm and skills pushed the mission into new and exciting areas.

One such volunteer was Jessie Luther, whom Wilfred met when he was on a lecture tour in New England. He visited a hospital in Marblehead, Massachusetts, and Jessie showed him around. Sometime before, she had been a patient at the hospital and was amazed at how boring a hospital stay could be. When she got well, she persuaded a doctor to allow her to start craft classes among the patients. She brought in weavers, knitters, and woodcarvers to teach the patients their skills. The doctor soon noticed that these busy patients were happier and healed faster. When Wilfred saw what Jessie had achieved, he invited her to come to St. Anthony and bring her ideas with her.

Jessie did come, and soon the hospital at St. Anthony had an industrial department attached to it that taught hooked-rug making, ivory and wood carving, weaving, moccasin and glove making, and the cutting and mounting of semiprecious stones. Soon the local people became involved too, and many housewives learned new skills and were able to supplement their families' incomes through the long winter months.

Wilfred's concern for the children had taken on a new form too. An orphanage was opened at St. Anthony, and Wilfred had the words of Jesus, "Suffer the little children to come unto Me," painted in large white letters along the roofline. An English volunteer, an old friend of Wilfred's named Eleanor Storr, came to Newfoundland to look after the first six children who were housed in the orphanage.

The only thing that could pull Wilfred away from the Labrador coast was the necessity to undertake speaking tours to raise increasingly larger amounts of money to keep the mission going.

It was Easter Sunday, April 19, 1908, and Wilfred was just leaving church in St. Anthony when a man came running up to him across the snow.

"Dr. Grenfell, Dr. Grenfell," the man called.

Wilfred stepped forward.

"Dr. Grenfell," the man said again, out of breath, "we have come from Brent Island in Hare Bay.

T'boy you operated on two weeks ago is very sick. It be blood poisoning, I believe. You must come there and help him."

Wilfred remembered the boy; he had operated on him for osteomyelitis. He immediately swung into action. "I will get there as quickly as I can," he said as he ran off to his house to gather up his things for the journey. Brent Island was sixty miles to the south, and it would take two days to get there.

Once his eight dogs had been attached to his komatik, Wilfred was on his way. He also took with him his retriever, Jack, a small black spaniel. Jack bounced along beside the komatik as they set off. It was agreed that the men who had come from Brent Island would stay and rest themselves and their dogs before setting out again.

By nightfall Wilfred had made it to the small village of Lock's Cove on the northern shore of Hare Bay. He spent the night with a family before setting out early the following morning.

During the night a stiff wind from the northeast had sprung up, causing the ice pack on the bay to break up into ice pans. Normally Wilfred would have set out with his komatik and dogs across the bay, taking the most direct route to Brent Island, which lay close to the south shore of Hare Bay. Since his route across the ice pack was blocked, Wilfred made his way down the shore of the bay.

Wilfred was several miles down the coast when he noticed that an ice bridge to a small uninhabited island in the bay was still intact. If he took the ice bridge to the island and then crossed the narrow sheet of ice between the island and the shore, he would cut a number of miles off his journey and arrive to treat his patient sooner. Wilfred called to his lead dog, Brin, who veered in the direction of the ice bridge, leading the other dogs behind him.

Soon Wilfred, riding on his komatik, was speeding across the ice bridge toward the island, the dogs barking as they raced along. All was going well until Wilfred noticed that they had ventured onto sish ice, a thick, gooey layer of ice formed when ice pans were buffeted together by the wind and small pieces broke off the edges. Suddenly the komatik began to sink into the sish ice, making it almost impossible for the dogs to pull the sled. As the dogs slowed down, they, too, began to sink into the sish ice.

Wilfred knew he had to do something, and fast. In an instant he leaped off the komatik, pulling out his knife at the same time. With a swish of his knife, he cut through the walrus-hide traces that held the dogs to the sled. The dogs pulled free, and Wilfred grabbed the cut traces and held on as tightly as he could. The dogs pulled him through the sish ice until finally Brin scrambled up onto a pan of ice. The other dogs followed, dragging Wilfred along with them.

Shivering and wet to the bone, Wilfred clambered onto the ice pan. He knew he did not have time to think about how cold he was—not if he wanted to survive. The ice pan they were on was too small and was already beginning to sink with him and nine dogs on it. To make matters worse, the wind had shifted. It was now blowing from the northwest and was blowing the ice pans out to sea and away from the coast.

Wilfred spotted another, larger ice pan about twenty yards away. *If only we could make it there,* he muttered to himself as he tied the dog traces around both wrists. He threw Brin into the water in the hope that he would swim to the larger ice pan and lead the other dogs there, pulling Wilfred with them. But Brin merely climbed back onto the ice pan he had been thrown from. Wilfred tried again and again, with the same result. Brin did not understand what Wilfred wanted him to do. Then he remembered Jack, his black spaniel retriever. Wilfred picked up a chunk of ice and threw it onto the larger ice pan. "Go fetch," he ordered Jack.

The spaniel sprang into action, sloshing its way across the sish ice to the ice pan.

"Stay," Wilfred commanded when the animal was safely across.

Seeing Jack standing on the ice pan, Brin suddenly got the idea. He leaped into the sish ice, the other dogs following him, tugging Wilfred along. A few minutes later they were all safely standing on an ice pan about ten feet by twelve feet.

Wilfred would have liked to make it to an even bigger ice pan another twenty yards away, but by now he was too cold, and he knew he had to get his body temperature up if he was to survive. He pulled off his wet clothing and wrung out each item. Then he put on one layer of clothing at a time and sat, trying to use his body heat to dry the various items of clothing. While he did not get them completely dry this way, he managed to get them to where they were damp but not sopping wet. As he sat drying his clothes, Wilfred took his fur moccasins that reached all the way up to his thighs and cut the tops off them just above the ankles. Then with his knife he split them open, and using some of the walrus hide from the dog traces, he stitched together a kind of cape that he could drape around his shoulders for warmth.

As he worked, the ice pan continued to be blown out across the bay. Wilfred knew that if it were blown all the way out to sea, he would never be rescued. The ice pan would be pounded to pieces by heavy sea, dumping him and the dogs into the frigid ocean and certain death. As it was, Wilfred knew his chance of survival was slim. Not only was cold now his greatest enemy, but the coastline of Hare Bay was uninhabited between Lock's Cove to the north and the coastal islands to the south. Even if the ice pan stayed in the bay, it was unlikely that anyone would see him and rescue him. But Wilfred would not let himself dwell on such things. Right now he needed to do all he could to survive.

The afternoon wore on, and with it, Wilfred's attempt to dry his clothes as much as he could. Then, as afternoon shadows stretched long across the bay and the temperature began to plummet, Wilfred knew he had to do more to stay warm. It dawned on him that he would have to do the unthinkable. He would have to kill some of the dogs and use their hides as a blanket against the biting cold. Wilfred thought about the grisly task for a while, but he could see no way around it.

Once he had killed three of the dogs, Wilfred used lengths of the walrus-hide traces to fashion the skins together into a blanket. The warmth he would receive had come at a high price.

By now it was completely dark, and Wilfred decided to try to see if he could get some sleep. He called his largest dog, Doc, to him and told the animal to lie down beside him. Wilfred then snuggled up to Doc for warmth, his dog-skin blanket pulled tightly around him.

Wilfred awoke several hours later, his fingers stinging from the cold. He thought he saw the sun rising, but when he looked closer, he realized that it was a bright, full moon peeking through the clouds above.

Once again Wilfred took up his position beside Doc for warmth. By now the dog was growling, thinking Wilfred was one of the other dogs wriggling beside him and waking him. Wilfred tried to lie as still as possible. As he tried to drift off to sleep once again, the words of a hymn that he had sung as a boy back in Parkgate began to play over and over in his mind.

> My God, my Father, while I stray
> Far from my home on life's dark way,
> Oh, teach me from my heart to say,
> Thy will be done!

Wilfred did not know how long he had slept this time, but he awoke with the same stinging cold fingers. This time, though, an idea was pulsing in his head. He needed a pole and flag. That way maybe, just maybe, someone onshore might spot him and rescue him. His spirits were buoyed when he realized the wind had died down and the ice pan was no longer floating out to sea. But he was still more than five miles out from the closest point of land on Hare Bay.

As he thought about a flagpole, Wilfred realized that his dogs' sacrifice would have to serve him yet again. It was not easy, but working in the dark, he at last managed to lash the dogs' leg bones together with lengths of walrus hide to form a pole.

By now the sun had risen. Wilfred pulled off his flannel shirt and attached it to the pole. He clambered to his feet and began to wave the pole above his head. It wasn't very tall, but at least it hoisted the flannel-shirt flag five feet farther into the air.

Wilfred waved as hard as he could. His arms throbbed, but he forced himself to carry on. He told himself that this was his last chance. If he stopped waving the flag right now, someone might come along onshore in five minutes and not see it and know that he was trapped out on an ice pan in the bay. He was cold, and he was hungry. He knew he could not survive more than twenty-four hours on the ice; he had to keep waving.

Eventually Wilfred could not will himself to wave any longer, and he had to sit and take a break. After twenty minutes he rose to his feet again. By now his feet and hands were so cold he could not feel them. They were simply lumps of flesh at the ends of his legs and arms that he willed to move in order to survive.

Again Wilfred waved the flagpole for as long as he could until once again he was forced to take a break.

The third time he stood waving the flagpole, he noticed something in the distance—the light from the bright morning sun was glinting off something. It was something that seemed to be moving up and down. Wilfred tried to focus on it, but the glare of the sun off the ice had partially blinded him. He kept waving at whatever it was in the distance. Slowly, ever so slowly, the moving object assumed the shape of oars and then the lines of a rowboat. It was a boat! Wilfred could scarcely believe it. Four men were rowing the boat, and a fifth was guiding them along the fissures in the ice.

"Doctor! You're alive! Stay where you are. We will come to you," one of the men called from the rowboat.

Half an hour later they were helping Wilfred into the boat. Tears streamed down the men's faces when they saw that he was safe. They wrapped him in a warm blanket and then poured him a cup of hot tea from a flask they had brought with them. Finally the six remaining dogs climbed into the boat, and the men began to row back to shore, following the fissures in the ice.

Once they were ashore, Wilfred was given warm clothes to change into and the best bowl of stew he had ever eaten. During the boat ride back to shore, nobody had said much, but now, with warm clothes on his body and warm food in his stomach, Wilfred began to talk, telling those who had gathered to wish him well about his ordeal and how he had managed to survive.

The men who had rescued Wilfred told him how lucky he was to be alive. Several men from the village had made a trip down the lonely coast to collect some seals they had killed earlier and had left hanging until they froze. One of the men had said he saw a man adrift on an ice pan far out on the bay. At first no one believed him, but when someone searched the bay with a spyglass, he spotted Wilfred adrift. But the wind then was too strong to launch a rescue attempt. The men had to wait until morning, all the while hoping that Wilfred would survive the night and not be blown out to sea.

The following day the men tied Wilfred onto a komatik and took him back to St. Anthony. Wilfred was eager to get back there and assure everyone that he was safe. Unfortunately, as his hands and feet thawed out, the pain was unbearable. His fingers and toes had suffered minor frostbite, and he could not walk or use his hands for much.

Wilfred was welcomed enthusiastically at St. Anthony. Many in the community were convinced he had died on the ice. When they saw him alive, they rushed to him and, with tears in their eyes, welcomed him home.

The boy from Brent Island, whom Wilfred had been on his way to help, arrived safely in St. Anthony two days later, the breakup of the ice allowing him passage across the bay by boat. His blood poisoning was treated at the hospital, and several days later he returned home to Brent Island, well on his way to making a full recovery.

Glad to be safely home, Wilfred was eager to be up and about again, but his frostbitten fingers and toes forced him to slow down while he recuperated. While he lay in bed recovering, Wilfred dictated an account of his ordeal on the ice to Jessie Luther, and this account was published as a book titled *Adrift on an Ice-Pan*.

Once he had fully recuperated, Wilfred set out on his usual summer activities, traveling up and down the Labrador coast in the *Strathcona*.

The following year Wilfred made a trip home to England. Much to his surprise, *Adrift on an Ice-Pan* had become a best-seller. Now when he spoke, bigger crowds than ever came to hear him. It seemed to Wilfred that everyone wanted to hear about his ordeal on the ice.

Chapter 14

International Grenfell Association

For the first time in his life, Wilfred was aboard a ship with his mother. Although she was now seventy-nine and a semi-invalid, she had jumped at the chance to sail to the United States to watch Wilfred accept two honorary degrees, one from Harvard University and one from Williams College. The year before, Wilfred had received an honorary doctorate of medicine from Oxford University. It was the first honorary medical degree ever issued by that institution.

For the voyage across the Atlantic Ocean, the president of the Cunard Line had kindly given Jane Grenfell the use of a luxurious suite of cabins, and she spent most of the voyage in them. Wilfred, on the other hand, was a ball of energy, inspecting the

Mauretania from stem to stern and befriending the captain and crew. On the second day of the voyage, he saw something that truly startled him. It was the sight of a female passenger. She was about twenty years younger than he, and for some reason, Wilfred could not take his eyes off her. He had been introduced to hundreds of beautiful women during his forty-four years, but there was something irresistible about this woman. Staring at her across the dining room, he decided to ask her at once to marry him.

The opportunity came that evening when Wilfred was walking around the deck. The young woman, dressed in black, was sitting on one of the deck chairs doing some embroidery. Wilfred sat down beside her.

"Excuse me, madam," he said. "I would like to ask you a question."

He watched as her eyebrows arched.

"Yes, go on," she replied.

Wilfred took a deep breath and blurted out, "Will you marry me?"

The young woman's hands flew to her face as she gasped. "But you don't even know my name!"

Wilfred nodded in agreement. "That is not the issue. The only issue that interests me is what your name is going to be."

"Don't be ridiculous!" she retorted. "Of course I will not consent to marry you, but I will have breakfast with you at nine o'clock sharp. I am traveling with the Stirling family; we will be in the aft dining room. By the way, my name is Miss Anne Elizabeth MacClanahan."

With that the woman folded her embroidery, put it into a satin bag, and walked off.

Wilfred sat for some time wondering what had come over him. Never in his entire life had he felt he needed a wife, and now he was smitten with a woman he did not know.

The following morning Wilfred was up bright and early pacing the deck, wondering whether he had made a complete fool of himself the night before. Thankfully, when nine o'clock came, Anne MacClanahan made him feel perfectly at ease as they breakfasted with her traveling companions. As the meal progressed, Wilfred found out more about her. She had grown up in Lake Forest, a wealthy suburb of Chicago. Her father, who had died when she was young, had been a colonel under Robert E. Lee in the Civil War. Her only sibling, a brother named Kinlock, had also died, leaving Anne's mother to raise her alone.

Anne had done the normal things that were expected of a girl of high social standing, complete with earning a bachelor's degree from Bryn Mawr. Now she was returning from a three-year tour of Europe.

Despite the rather impulsive beginning, Wilfred and Anne found that they liked each other, and by the time they disembarked in New York, Anne had promised to think about marrying Wilfred. She invited him and his mother to Chicago to meet her mother. Wilfred eagerly changed his plans to do this. But first he went to Williams College and then on to Harvard University and accepted his honorary degrees. As always, he used the opportunity to talk about the work in Labrador. He challenged the students at each university to become WOPS, giving a summer to serve their fellow human beings in the far north.

Finally it was time to head west to visit Anne MacClanahan and her mother. After two days together, Anne agreed to marry Wilfred. The wedding was set for November 18, 1909, two weeks away. Wilfred could not see any sense in waiting, especially since he had already been away from St. Anthony longer than he had intended.

The wedding was a quiet, formal affair at Grace Episcopal Church, followed by a honeymoon at Virginia Hot Springs. Then Wilfred and Anne Grenfell escorted his mother back to New York and put her back on a Cunard liner bound for England.

In January Wilfred wound up his speaking engagements, and the newlyweds headed north for the rest of the winter. Although Wilfred was sure that many people would wonder whether a Chicago socialite could survive the harsh conditions at St. Anthony, he had no such doubts. He was sure that Anne would adjust to whatever situation she found herself in, and he looked forward to introducing her to the life he loved.

Wilfred was having a house built for him while he was away, and he wrote to the carpenters asking them to add a few extra things that Anne had suggested. The result was stunning. Wilfred and Anne soon found themselves living in a lovely, two-story home overlooking the bay at St. Anthony. Within a year the house was filled with the sounds of a baby, Wilfred Jr.

Even though Anne had a son to look after, she took an active role in the mission, overseeing the child welfare department and starting an educational fund. The education of the children weighed on her the most. Using her numerous connections in the United States, Anne was able to arrange for boys and girls who graduated from the mission's schools to be sent off to colleges in Nova Scotia, Canada, and the United States. It was a huge task to outfit the students, buy their tickets, arrange scholarships, and settle them in at college. More often than not, Anne accompanied the students herself, though at times her assistant went with them.

Married life did not change Wilfred's routine much at all. Anne was quite capable of keeping things running on the homefront, and Wilfred was free to do his usual round of doctor visits. One project in particular consumed a lot of his time. It was the Seaman's Institute being built in St. John's. The institute contained dining halls, bedrooms, and a meeting hall that would seat three hundred. It was a place where fishermen and seamen could find somewhere to stay and eat when they were in St. John's without having to go to the local hotels and taverns. The institute had been a dream of Wilfred's for some time, and by 1911 he had raised the 170,000 dollars needed to build the facility, and work on the building was ready to begin.

The official ceremony to lay the cornerstone for the Seaman's Institute was held in June 1911. Wilfred excitedly attended the ceremony, which was held on the same day that George V, the new king of England, was crowned. The new king had lent his support to the project as patron, which had brought great media exposure for the mission. Following his coronation, George V pushed a button in England that sent a signal over the new transatlantic cable that emerged from the ocean at St. John's. The signal set a mechanical device into action, raising the Union Jack and moving the cornerstone down a ramp and into the ground. The crowd that had gathered for the ceremony went wild when the flag began to go up and the cornerstone began to move. After the ceremony, work on building the Seaman's Institute began in earnest.

With the building of the Seaman's Institute under way, Wilfred had another challenge ahead of him. This one had to do with the structure of the mission itself.

For many years now, Wilfred had been aware that his work in Labrador was much wider than the mandate of the original National Mission to Deep-Sea Fishermen. Most of the money that came in to finance Wilfred's work did not come directly from the mission in England but came from independent groups operating throughout the United States and Canada. These groups gave generously to the work among the Liveyeres of Labrador and the settlers in Newfoundland.

In his heart Wilfred knew it was time to cut loose from the mission in England and allow his work to stand on its own. In 1912, just after the birth of his second son, Pascoe, Wilfred decided to go to England to sort things out. Just as he was about to leave in April, Wilfred heard some stunning news. The unsinkable SS *Titanic* had hit an iceberg and had sunk four hundred miles off the coast of Newfoundland. One thousand five hundred passengers and crew had lost their lives in the icy ocean. Once again Wilfred was reminded of just how much a captain had to respect the changing moods of the North Atlantic.

England was in shock and mourning when Wilfred arrived. Many people could not accept that a ship like the *Titanic*, on her maiden voyage, could actually have sunk. Everywhere he went, Wilfred was asked questions about conditions off Newfoundland.

When Wilfred finally got to meet with the mission committee, tensions ran high. Each committee member seemed to have a different idea about what should happen with the work in Labrador and Newfoundland. Despite the tension, agreement was finally reached. The International Grenfell Association (IGA) would be incorporated. Wilfred would be the chairman of the new association, and its board would be drawn from members of the many groups that supported the work. The Royal National Mission to Deep-Sea Fishermen agreed to contribute two thousand pounds a year over the next five years toward supporting the work among the fishermen.

Wilfred was greatly relieved once everything was settled. Now he could move ahead with lots of new plans. And move ahead he did.

Wilfred arrived back in St. Anthony in time for the opening of the new Seaman's Institute. The official opening ceremony was held on June 22, 1912. Wilfred got up steam in the *Strathcona* to sail to St. John's for the ceremony, but before he could get under way, he was asked for help. The previous year a fishing schooner had sunk off the Labrador coast. In early summer the captain and owner of the schooner and his crew of fishermen had reached the site where the vessel went down. Amazingly they had managed to float the boat again. They patched the leaking hull with bags of ship's biscuits soaked in water, cement, and planking. They then sailed the schooner sixty miles south, where they put into a small harbor where a number of other fishing boats were at anchor. At the harbor, officials told the captain that he could sail no farther because his boat was unsafe.

The captain of the schooner came to see Wilfred and asked if he would tow the boat to St. John's, where it could be repaired. Of course Wilfred was eager to be on his way to the opening of the Seaman's Institute, but he also had compassion for the captain and his crew. If they could not get their boat to St. John's to be repaired, they would miss the whole fishing season. That meant that the fishermen's families would be left to face winter without money to buy the necessary supplies to tide them over. Wilfred steamed to the harbor and took the schooner in tow. If he missed the opening of the institute, so be it. These fishermen, whom he had come to Labrador to serve in the first place, needed help, and he would help them.

Fortunately, sailing conditions down the coast of Newfoundland island were good, and Wilfred sailed into St. John's Harbor just in time for the official opening of the Seaman's Institute.

The new red-brick building stood four stories high on Water Street, the main street of St. John's. It sat across the road from the spot where in 1583 Sir Humphrey Gilbert had come ashore and claimed Newfoundland island in the name of Queen Elizabeth I as England's first overseas colony.

Wilfred stood proudly as the building was officially opened and letters from King George V in England and President Taft in the United States commemorating the occasion were read.

Under the auspices of the International Grenfell Association, the work in Labrador and Newfoundland grew and flourished. By 1914 six doctors and eighteen nurses were on the permanent mission staff, and the numbers swelled to twenty doctors in the summer. Some of these doctors were world-renowned specialists who came to give their time to the mission. Six thousand patients were treated annually in the four hospitals and six nursing stations along the coast. Over 150 other WOPS came too. Many of them were teachers, accountants, plumbers, and carpenters who worked alongside the local people and taught them valuable skills. A growing number of single women volunteers were coming to look after the thirty children now at the orphanage.

In other ways, though, 1914 was a difficult year for Wilfred and the mission. Lord Strathcona,

Wilfred's friend and leading supporter, died suddenly. His will made provision for the mission to continue receiving one thousand pounds a year from his estate.

Then, in August, England went to war against Germany, and many of the IGA's staff left to join the war effort. The Moravian missionaries, many of whom were of German birth, were ordered out of Labrador, and the International Grenfell Association took on the responsibility of continuing their work among the Eskimos in the north.

In 1915 Wilfred felt he should do what he could to help with the war effort. Although he was fifty years old, he signed up to be part of the Harvard University medical unit that was going to France to help take care of the soldiers' medical needs. Wilfred was especially interested in treating soldiers with trench foot, a condition caused by the cold and wet. Within six months of arriving in France, there were more than enough volunteer doctors. Because of his age, Wilfred was discharged, and he returned to St. Anthony to continue his work.

When the war finally came to an end in 1918, an epidemic was sweeping across the world, demanding more of Wilfred and his workers than anything before ever had.

Chapter 15

Knight Commander of St. Michael and St. George

Influenza! The word struck fear into Wilfred and the other doctors and nurses at St. Anthony. The Great War had ended, and millions of people came together to celebrate. Unfortunately these great rallies had passed a deadly strain of influenza from person to person until it affected the entire world. Even the remotest regions of Labrador were not spared. Each day grisly reports arrived on Wilfred's desk. In the far north at Okkak, where 270 people lived, 231 of them had perished from the epidemic. Whole families had died within hours of each other. Their huts, with the bodies still inside, were burned to the ground in a futile attempt to stop the infection from spreading. Not a man was left alive in the settlement, and most of the surviving women and children were extremely weak. Wilfred dispatched a nurse to go and help them.

In one isolated cove a woman watched her entire family die, but she was too scared to leave her hut because ferocious, hungry sled dogs paced outside, ready to attack her. A medical team rescued her eleven days after the last death in the hut.

The doctors and nurses of the mission worked tirelessly to bring what little help they could to the influenza victims. Wilfred stayed in St. Anthony to coordinate the effort, turning the entire settlement into a hospital. Thankfully, no one in his family, including his year-old daughter, Rosamund, contracted the disease.

By 1920 the epidemic was over, and when the numbers were tallied, it was found that influenza had caused the death of over fifty million people worldwide.

Wilfred and the mission struggled to deal with the aftereffects of the epidemic along the coast. Widows were relocated to St. John's, and another orphanage was built at Cartwright, on the Labrador coast, to house and care for seventy orphaned children.

There were numerous other building needs, too. The hospital at St. Anthony needed to be rebuilt in stone, and a new hospital was needed at North West River, as well as nursing stations at Flower's Cove and Cartwright. The mission now owned six ships, which had all been donated for the work. It was up to the International Grenfell Association, however, to maintain, fuel, and equip them. Wilfred did not worry about any of this. He had built the mission with faith that God would provide for their needs, and he believed that God would continue to do so. The IGA council, though, was more concerned with the practical question of how God would do this.

Eventually the council came up with a plan to raise an endowment fund to continue Wilfred's work long after he had died. To achieve this, the council asked Wilfred to raise one and a half million dollars that it could invest. The interest from this amount would help to pay the costs of running the mission. Wilfred could see the logic in what the council was asking. He turned fifty-five in 1920 and knew he was the mission's best fundraiser. Still, the idea of spending many months raising money did not appeal to him at all. He wrote to his mother:

> It seems almost absurd, but the decision to reconcile myself to the facing of this task was perhaps the greatest effort I have ever made....The long fall cruise I had hoped to make in a renovated *Strathcona* must be abandoned, and the work on the sea I love must once more for the time give place to the raising of money.

Once he had made up his mind to raise the endowment, Wilfred and Anne had some difficult decisions to make. Their older son, Wilfred Jr., was nine years old now, and Anne wanted him to have a formal education in preparation for attending a good English college. The Grenfells decided to move their family to Brookline, a suburb of Boston, while Wilfred traveled the country to raise money.

A week before they were due to leave St. Anthony, a telegraph arrived at the hospital.

"Dr. Grenfell," it read. "Do your best to come and operate me I have an abscess under right tonsil will give you coal for your steamer am getting pretty weak. Captain J. N. Coté. Long Point."

Captain Coté was a lighthouse keeper at a Canadian lighthouse located one hundred miles away at the south end of the Strait of Belle Isle on the Quebec side. As quickly as he could, Wilfred got up steam in the *Strathcona* and set off to help Captain Coté.

It was late afternoon when they rounded the northern tip of Newfoundland island and into a howling gale. Even with a full head of steam up, the *Strathcona* could make no headway against the wind, and Wilfred was eventually forced to take shelter in a bay and drop anchor overnight.

The following morning the gale had subsided, and the *Strathcona* got under way again. She steamed on through the Strait of Belle Isle and made her way to the Quebec side. Once the crew spotted the lighthouse, the *Strathcona* maneuvered as close to it as possible. The ship was about one hundred feet from the lighthouse when a small motorboat was lowered into the water to bring Captain Coté from the lighthouse to the *Strathcona*. Water crashed over the rocks around the lighthouse as the small motorboat gingerly made her way toward the small lighthouse jetty. Captain Coté waited on the jetty, and as soon as the boat was close enough, he clambered onto it. Minutes later he was in surgery on the *Strathcona*.

Wilfred administered a local anaesthetic to the lighthouse keeper and then set to work removing the abscess at the back of his throat, which was obstructing his breathing. Captain Coté thanked Wilfred profusely for coming to his aid, and the Canadian government gave Wilfred four and a half tons of coal to replace the coal he had burned getting the *Strathcona* to the lighthouse. Then it was back to St. Anthony.

Once the Grenfell family had relocated from St. Anthony and was settled in Brookline, Wilfred set off on a whirlwind tour of the United States. He was a famous man now, and everyone wanted to hear him speak. He would speak as many as three times a day in halls and churches overflowing with listeners. He was welcomed by President Harding to the White House and received in the wealthiest homes in the country.

At the end of three months, Wilfred had raised half a million dollars, and by year's end that total had risen to nearly eight hundred thousand dollars. Prominent organizations promised to hold annual fundraisers for the International Grenfell Association. One of them, the Metropolitan Opera House in New York City, sent off a check for nine thousand dollars and promised a similar amount for the years that followed.

The next spring Wilfred was back in St. Anthony working on his next project. It was dubbed "Grenfell's Folly" by many who had heard about it, but Wilfred was sure his idea to build a first-class dry dock at the settlement would work.

Until this time the only dry docks where ships could be pulled from the water to have their hulls repaired were at St. John's. Many of the ships sailing in the northern regions were so badly damaged by storms or by collisions with rocks that there was no way they could make it to St. John's to be repaired. Believing that having a dry dock at St. Anthony was the next step in helping the fishermen, Wilfred prayed and planned for it to become a reality. In summer he received word that an anonymous donor had given money especially for the project, and work on building it was soon under way.

When it was finished, the dry dock was able to accommodate ships up to 150 feet long. The dry dock not only helped save many fishing schooners but also provided a source of income for the men who worked on the boats over the winter. Far from being a folly, the dry dock turned out to be a welcome addition to the village.

The year 1921 turned out to be a year of memories for Wilfred. His mother, who was ninety-one years old, died that year. She had been an invalid for many years, and although Wilfred was glad to think that her suffering was over, he knew he would miss her long, encouraging letters.

That year Wilfred's faithful ship, the *Strathcona*, sank as she crossed Bonavista Bay, on the Newfoundland coast. Wilfred was not aboard when she went down, but her end had been described to him, and he relived it in his mind many times. The sinking occurred as the *Strathcona* was crossing the bay under a strong northwest wind and heavy seas. As the vessel moved along, she began to fill with water. The captain, William Sims, asked a nearby schooner to stand by, and the schooner captain came aboard and surveyed the state of the ship. He urged Captain Sims to abandon the *Strathcona*. Reluctantly Captain Sims agreed that nothing could be done to save her. The *Strathcona* was too old and weakened to withstand the onslaught. The crew wept quietly as they climbed from the ship and onto the schooner. Half an hour later the *Strathcona* listed to port and sank.

It was a hard blow for Wilfred. He and the *Strathcona* had been traveling companions for nearly twenty-two years, and he admired her toughness. He wrote a newsletter explaining the loss. In it he said:

> How many busy days we have shared together, how many ventures we have essayed. How many times her decks have been crowded with our brethren seeking healing of the body—relief from pain—counsel in anxiety. Babes have been born on board her, helpless children saved and carried to

the permanent care of loving hands. Some have been married and others have died in her accommodating shelter.... Once she towed nineteen shipwrecked crews to safety; once she saved from a wreck nearly two hundred persons. Five times she has been on the rocks herself.... Many have gathered in her cabin for worship and praise.... A thousand times the sound of her whistle and the flutter of her flags have brought to eager, waiting hearts the message of hope and help.

Wilfred and the *Strathcona* were both legends on the Labrador coast, and as Wilfred lamented the sinking of the ship, he could not help thinking he was beginning to lose some of his usefulness to the mission as well. He continued to do what he could, but he was not as well as he once had been. His blood pressure soared, and he suffered from headaches and heart palpitations. In 1926, while climbing a hill in Labrador, Wilfred suffered a heart attack. It was not enough to kill him, but it did give him a scare. He returned to Boston to recover, and bad news awaited him there. Anne had been diagnosed with stomach cancer. As a result, the ailing couple decided to move to a house in Vermont on the shore of Lake Champlain, where they could retire together.

Wilfred soon recovered from his heart attack, and although he was pleased to be in Vermont for Anne's sake, he was sorry to be so far from the sea.

He bought a sixteen-foot yacht and sailed it on the lake, but it was no substitute for being on the gray, restless sea.

Anne was under the care of the best specialists, and after the initial crisis, she seemed much better. Her friend Eleanor Cushman, the Grenfells' secretary, agreed to stay with her as long as she was needed. This freed Wilfred up to travel once again, and in the spring of 1927, he headed back to St. Anthony for a special event—the opening of the new, large, brick hospital building.

Just as he had with the opening of the Seaman's Institute at St. John's fifteen years before, Wilfred almost missed the event! He had taken the *Strathcona*'s replacement, the *Strathcona II*, north to tend to a fisherman's wife who was very ill. On the way south again, they encountered heavy fog. Wilfred, who was standing on deck at the time, heard the sickening sound of grinding metal. In the fog the ship had struck the rocks. The waves beat relentlessly over her bow, and Wilfred could do nothing but hail a passing ship and ask that he and the crew be transferred onto it.

By the time Wilfred scrambled to safety, the *Strathcona II* was listing dangerously. Wilfred asked the schooner captain to stay nearby until she sank. Amazingly this did not happen. Wilfred watched as the unmanned hospital ship floated clear of the rocks on the high tide. Although she still listed precariously, Wilfred began to wonder if she might not be repairable. He asked the captain to return him to the ship, where he found everything inside smashed but her hull still intact. The *Strathcona II* would live to sail another day, after all!

The pumps were blocked with coal, so Wilfred and the crew bailed water out of the ship using a bucket brigade. Once enough water had been bailed out, the boilers were lit, and the ship limped back to St. Anthony, escorted by several schooners.

They arrived on July 24, the day before the opening ceremony of the new hospital building. Everyone else, including the governor of Newfoundland, Sir William Allardyce, and his wife, was already there. The ceremony was a moving experience, perhaps most of all for Wilfred. He recalled when he spent his first winter at St. Anthony. He had played soccer on the ice and encouraged the locals to think of themselves as a community. Together they had cut down the trees for the original hospital building, hardly daring to imagine that something so vital could happen in their bay. Now St. Anthony was a thriving hub of activity, with its cottage industries, dry dock, and state-of-the-art hospital.

The community was in good spirits too. Wilfred looked out over the St. Anthony Church Boys' Brigade and the mission's Boy Scouts and Girl Guides as they formed an honor parade for him. Salutes were fired from the HMS *Wistaria*, the Royal Navy ship that had brought the dignitaries north from St. John's.

It was a proud day for Wilfred, though he had no idea that another ceremony besides the opening of the hospital building had been planned. After Sir William Allardyce officially opened the hospital building and cut the ribbon, he turned to Wilfred and said with great pomp, "His Majesty, King George V, is pleased to confer the honor of Knight Commander of St. Michael and St. George on Dr. Grenfell."

Wilfred gasped. He was now Sir Wilfred Grenfell.

Chapter 16

Home at Last

Wilfred's new title seemed to open a floodgate of honors for him. He found himself accepted as a fellow of the Royal Geographical Society, he was a guest at the British prime minister's home, and he was a welcomed friend at the royal palace. Prominent English businessmen sought him out for advice, and duchesses organized flower shows to aid his cause.

Wilfred was never impressed with the honors themselves, but he was grateful for the doors they opened for him and the International Grenfell Association. His place in the Royal Geographical Society led to the fulfillment of another of Wilfred's ambitions, this time to map the entire coast of Labrador. Accurate maps would save many fishermen's lives and make fishing itself more profitable. Wilfred approached the British Air Ministry for an aircraft to carry out the survey, and although it was sympathetic, it could not spare the men or machines to help.

Once again Wilfred turned to the United States. He had a friend, a Harvard professor by the name of Alexander Forbes, who owned both an airplane and a motorized schooner. Wilfred persuaded Forbes to lend them both to the project. The Royal Geographical Society endorsed the charting, and the Newfoundland government agreed to carry all freight associated with the project free of charge and to waive all customs fees and licenses.

In the spring of 1931, Wilfred sat in the cockpit of Forbes's airplane, peering out over the landscape that he knew so well from an ocean perspective. The pilot swooped and dipped the wings as the plane flew over mountains, fjords, cascading waterfalls, and the tiny settlements that clung to the rocky coastline.

Slowly, accurate readings showing rocky outcrops, shoals, water depths, and dangerous bluffs emerged. The information was sent off to the New York Geographical Society, which had offered to turn the data into maps and charts. By the end of the year, many fishermen along the coast had access to more information than had ever before been available.

Still Wilfred pressed on. For every task he completed, he thought of five more he should start. He and the other doctors had long been concerned about the nutrition of the people who lived on the coast.

Many of the people suffered from beriberi, a disease caused by lack of a B-vitamin found in vegetables. In fact, there were no vegetables grown on the coast; everyone argued that the growing season was too short. And they were right. But a short growing season was just another challenge to Wilfred Grenfell, who exclaimed, "If the season is too short, we'll make it longer!"

At first people laughed at Wilfred, but they stopped once prefabricated greenhouses started arriving in St. Anthony. Wilfred, in his usual persuasive manner, had convinced many American garden clubs to donate greenhouses, plants, and seed to the mission. The greenhouses allowed the plants to get a three-month head start on spring so that by the time the weather was warm enough to set the plants outside, the plants were strong, healthy, and half-grown. The project was an instant success, as eighteen-pound cabbages and handfuls of plump carrots were proudly displayed in the community rooms.

In 1932 fifteen thousand hothouse plants were sold to local people up and down the coast. The tide of poor nutrition was beginning to turn at last.

During 1932 Wilfred suffered a mild stroke, which, along with his heart attack, reminded him that his strength was beginning to fail.

In 1934 he visited England again, where he was entertained by the Duke and Duchess of York, who would soon become King George VI and Queen Elizabeth. The royal couple heartily endorsed the International Grenfell Association and attended a fundraiser at the Royal Theatre in the association's honor.

While in England Wilfred visited his brother Algernon. The two brothers, both of them old and gray by now, sat on the lawn of Mostyn House School, looking out over the estuary of the River Dee and reliving the wonderful fishing and hunting trips they had enjoyed sixty years before. The fishing boats were all gone now; the estuary had silted up, meaning that the neap tides no longer splashed over the brick embankment.

Wilfred also visited his son Pascoe. Wilfred Jr. had graduated two years earlier from Oxford University, but Pascoe was still studying at Cambridge. Finally it was time to head "home" from England to Vermont, to see Anne.

Anne was doing as well as could be expected. At times her pain was great and she was unable to do much, but at other times she traveled and spoke to raise money for the endowment fund.

In Vermont Wilfred found himself in a forced retirement. He filled his days as best he could. He swam in the lake every morning, went for long hikes, sketched birds, and caught butterflies, but he was never truly happy away from the smell of salt water. He wrote countless letters to people he remembered in Labrador, often enclosing a check if he thought they might be in a difficult spot. Many of the staff wrote to him regularly, keeping him up to date on the goings-on at the hospitals and the latest research they were applying to their work.

Still, by 1937 Wilfred knew he was too far out of touch to any longer be an effective leader of the International Grenfell Association, and he resigned as superintendent of the association. The board wrote back informing him that he would now be officially known as the founder and that his ideas and suggestions would always be welcomed and considered.

The following year, in October 1938, Anne's doctors advised her to have another operation. The Grenfells, along with two nurses and a secretary, set out for Boston. The operation to remove a tumor from Anne's stomach was not supposed to be high-risk, but Anne developed complications and slowly slipped away. As Anne grew weaker, Wilfred wrote to a friend. "Now that the final goal seems not so far away, we are holding hands closer than ever, confident that the final experience of life also will be easier to face then and indeed become another joyous adventure, when these worn-out bodily machines of ours shall be discarded, and on the other side we shall work again in a new field together."

Lady Anne Grenfell died on December 9, 1938.

For the first time in many years, Wilfred had nothing in particular to do and no one in particular to do it with. After Anne's funeral he went south to St. Simon Island, in Georgia, and then on to Miami, where he stayed at Dr. Kellogg's health clinic. Many people still recognized him, and he could draw an extraordinary crowd. The Pan-American League, which was holding a conference in Miami, invited Wilfred to speak to them. Over four thousand people showed up to hear what he had to say. For the first time, Wilfred found himself a little befuddled in front of the crowd. He later wrote to a friend, "I was quite nervous the night before and I never had been that way before until lately. What is happening to my old think box I do not know, but I forget words. I have never had such a fight to give the message I wanted."

Wilfred knew that his speaking days were numbered, and for the first time in his life, he was content to think of spending the winter quietly at home beside the lake. However, during the winter he came up with a new idea. Anne had asked to be cremated, and Wilfred decided to take her ashes back to St. Anthony to be buried. The thought of seeing his old friends invigorated him, and he set about making plans for what he was sure would be his last trip north.

In July 1939 Wilfred was on board a ship once again. This time it was a tourist ship sailing from Montreal up the coast to Labrador. With him were his daughter, Rosamund, his personal assistant, Wyman Shaw, and another old friend from Georgia. It did not take long for word to spread that Sir Wilfred Grenfell was on board, and the passengers flocked to get his autograph and hear him reminisce. Many passengers confided that they had come on the tour as a result of hearing Wilfred speak years before or because they had read one of the many books he had written describing his adventures in Labrador. This alone made Wilfred happy that he had come. For many years he had tried to get tourism going in Labrador, but it had not been possible until the coast was properly charted and safe for tourists.

Wilfred arrived in St. Anthony on August 31, 1939. It had been five long years since he had seen the village. Hundreds of people were waiting patiently on the pier for him. They cheered and waved evergreen tree boughs to welcome him. Wilfred, with Rosamund on his arm, disembarked from the ship and walked slowly up the path that led to the hospital. Memories flooded his mind as he looked into the faces of so many colleagues and friends.

Wilfred stayed in his old house, which was now being used by Dr. Charlie Curtis, the new superintendent of the mission and the doctor in charge of the St. Anthony Hospital. When Wilfred had rested, Dr. Curtis took him on a tour of the settlement. They inspected the cavernous barns where dairy herds wintered over and the rows of greenhouses that supplied the hospital with fresh vegetables. Wilfred visited with the disabled fishermen who now made adequate livings carving ivory and polishing labradorite, a local semiprecious stone, and the women and children who made garments out of deerskin.

Wilfred strolled through the school and orphanage, recalling the seventy children who had been orphaned as a result of the influenza epidemic of 1919. It was hard for him to believe that that was twenty years ago. Dr. Curtis left the best for last: he took Wilfred on a tour of the hospital, which had been expanded since the last time Wilfred had seen it and now had two hundred beds. The equipment and care Wilfred saw rivaled anything he had seen in the best hospitals in Boston, an observation that made him proud. He had always said that God intended to give the people of Labrador the very best, and they certainly had it.

On the second day, Wilfred, Rosamund, and their friends held a service to remember Anne and lay her ashes to rest. The spot Wilfred chose was high on a hill overlooking the cove and the home she and Wilfred had shared. It was a moving moment for Wilfred as he recalled how Anne had made his mission her own as well.

Dr. Curtis had a special treat in store for Wilfred. He gave him command of the *Northern Messenger,* one of the mission's tenders, and told him he could take it where he pleased. With an engineer, a pilot, and his companions, Wilfred set off across the Belle Isle Strait to Red Bay. As he took the helm, the years seemed to fall away, and Wilfred was once again that twenty-seven-year-old seeing the Labrador coast for the first time.

Red Bay, the site of the first cooperative society on the coast, had prospered. Many people remembered Wilfred, and those who were too young to do so had heard many tales about his kindness and courage.

When he returned to St. Anthony, Wilfred was invited on a cruise to Hare Bay. Once again the memories flooded back. This time he was on the ice pan, floating out to sea, with only his dogs for company and his faith to keep him from giving up hope.

Finally, in late August, it was time for Wilfred to board the steamer and head south. Everyone in St. Anthony came to see him off. They sang "Auld Lang Syne" as the steamer pulled away, and Wilfred took off his hat and waved it at everyone. It had been the most extraordinary visit of his life, and he was glad he had lived long enough to see so many of his plans come to fruition. He wiped his eyes as the music faded and the ship steamed out into the open ocean.

Back in the United States, Wilfred kept himself busy, though his mind often wandered back to those special days that summer. He attended an alumni dinner in New York City, where 250 former WOPS came together to raise money and greet their beloved leader. Over thirty-five hundred WOPS had gone out to serve with the mission over the years, and Wilfred knew that they had played a significant role in propelling the mission forward. Then Wilfred took a train across the country to accept an honorary degree from the University of California, lecturing at various stops as he went.

Wilfred was back in Vermont when the Second World War broke out. He recalled his days in France in 1915, and it upset him to think that another round of bloodshed was in store for Europe. He had no thought of visiting England again, as Algernon had died the year before, but he kept up with the news on a daily basis.

On the afternoon of Wednesday, October 9, 1940, Wilfred played croquet with some visitors. After the match he felt tired and excused himself and went up to his room for a nap before dinner. He drifted off to sleep with his mind full of plans for the International Grenfell Association. An hour later he was dead.

News of Sir Wilfred Grenfell's death reverberated around the world like the salute of a battleship's cannon. Wilfred's funeral, which was held in Boston, was a huge ceremony, complete with representatives of the king of England and the governments of the United States, Canada, and Newfoundland. But it was the simple ceremony a year later, on that rugged hill above St. Anthony, that reflected the life Wilfred had chosen. Aged fishermen, doctors, nurses, orphaned children, and two blind twins all stood arm in arm singing Wilfred's favorite hymns as they placed his ashes into the stone vault. Below them, the North Atlantic Ocean crashed against the rocks. Wilfred was home at last.

Bibliography

Grenfell, Wilfred T. *Adrift on an Ice-Pan.* Houghton Mifflin Company, 1909.

Johnston, James. *Grenfell of Labrador.* S. W. Partridge & Co., 1908.

Kerr, J. Lennox. *Wilfred Grenfell: His Life and Work.* Dodd, Mead & Company, 1959.

Martin, R. G. *Knight of the Snows: The Story of Wilfred Grenfell.* G. R. Welch Company, Ltd., 1966.

Mathews, Basil. *Wilfred Grenfell the Master Mariner: A Life of Adventure on Sea and Ice.* George H. Doran Company, 1924.

Miller, Basil. *Wilfred Grenfell: Labrador's Dogsled Doctor.* Zondervan Publishing House, 1948.

About the Authors

Janet and Geoff Benge are a husband and wife writing team with more than thirty years of writing experience. Janet is a former elementary school teacher. Geoff holds a degree in history. Originally from New Zealand, the Benges spent ten years serving with Youth With A Mission. They have two daughters, Laura and Shannon, and an adopted son, Lito. They make their home in the Orlando, Florida, area.

CHRISTIAN HEROES: THEN & NOW are available in paperback, e-book, and audiobook formats, with more coming soon!

www.YWAMpublishing.com